AS YOU WERE
MEMOIRS OF WW II

BY
WILLIAM M. CRAIGHEAD
AND
KINGDON W. SWAYNE

ACCLAIM PRESS
MORLEY, MISSOURI

Acclaim Press
—— *Your Next Great Book* ——
P.O. Box 238
Morley, Missouri 63767
(573) 472-9800
www.acclaimpress.com

Publishing Consultant: Keith Steele

Library of Congress Control Number: 2007926050

ISBN: 978-0-9790025-7-1

First Printing 2007
Printed in the United States of America
10 9 8 7 6 5 4 3 2 1

TABLE OF CONTENTS

On the Home Front:

Signing of Treaty:

Appendix

DEDICATION

To Those

Who Made

the

Supreme Sacrifice

COVER DESIGN

Roger Cook is an internationally known graphic designer, photographer and artist. Cook is a graduate of the Pratt Institute and in 1997 was selected as Alumnus of the Year. He has also served on the Pratt Advisory Board and has been a member of the American Institute of Graphic Arts.

In 2003, "Symbols Signs," a project designed by his firm for the United States Department of Transportation, was accepted by the Acquisitions Committee to the collections of Cooper Hewitt, National Design Museum, Smithsonian Institution.

On January 30, 1984, Roger Cook received the Presidential Award for Design Excellence from President Reagan and Elizabeth Dole in the Indian Treaty Room of the Old Executive Office Building in Washington, D.C..

Roger is retired, and lives with his wife in Washington Crossing, Pennsylvania.

The title, "As You Were," a common military term used in all branches of the services, was suggested by the designer of the cover, Roger Cook.

ACKNOWLEDGEMENTS

The authors wish to recognize the many people who agreed to be interviewed about their war-time experiences. For each there is a short biography that includes their family, profession, service to their community, and in some cases, how their lives may have been influenced by the war.

Though most of those interviewed live in Newtown, Pennsylvania, others come from other places in the United States.

It is our regret that more of the local veterans were not interviewed. It has been more than three years since we undertook this project. Of the 65 interviewed, seven have already died.

We also want to give special thanks and appreciation to the following people:

Carole Davis, for transcribing to hard copy the many tapes used in this document, making this book possible.

Johnny Craighead for his significant contribution in researching the life and work of his father, John Craighead and his uncle, Frank Craighead.

Virginia Lloyd, a high school classmate and alumna of the same institution of both authors, for her thorough editing of the text and most of the interviews.

Dan Wolfe, for providing some special pictures for the text, in particular the signing of the Peace Treaty, September 2, 1945, aboard the *USS Missouri* in Tokyo Bay.

Bob Anderson, for his interest and expertise in the write-up on Don Hopkins, who was at Pearl Harbor during the attack.

John Davis, for his expert advice and help in the use of the computer to produce the final draft of this book.

INTRODUCTION

This collection of the memories of veterans of World War II and a few others is the work of two veterans of that war. Both are residents of Newtown, Pennsylvania and both are graduates and some-time employees of George School, a Quaker secondary school in Newtown, Pennsylvania.

They undertook the task in the early years of the 21st century as a gift to their Newtown neighbors and the latters' descendants. Others have persuaded them that it is a gift that should be shared with a wider audience. While most of the veterans whose stories are told here are residents of Newtown, their experiences of World War II are representative of the lives of millions of American soldiers who fought, and sometimes died, for their country in that war.

These are accounts of the personal experiences of people now in their seventies or eighties, experiences that will soon be lost to future generations if not recorded and published now. These stories mostly constitute tape recordings of conversations between the authors and the individuals interviewed. In some cases they have been recorded by telephone. A few are the result of their own written accounts. In other cases stories have been researched or verified from the Internet for accuracy, spelling, and detail.

The authors express their appreciation to the many veterans and others who were willing to be interviewed. We trust that the interpretations of these interviews remain faithful to the original conversation.

WW II — CHRONOLOGY
EUROPEAN AND PACIFIC THEATRES

<u>1933</u>   Both Germany and Japan leave the League of Nations.

<u>1936</u>   **Italy annexes Ethiopia**, Spanish Civil War begins, and **Germany remilitarizes the Rhine,** in violation of the **Versailles Treaty**. Germany establishes alliances with both Italy and Japan.

<u>1937</u>   Italy leaves the League of Nations and joins Germany and Japan in the **Anti-Comintern Pact**.

<u>1938</u>   Hitler persuades British, French and Italian leaders to support Germany's **annexation** of the **Sudetenland**.

<u>1939</u>   Hungary and Manchukuo in <u>February</u> and Spain in <u>March</u> join the Anti-Comintern Pact. Hitler, speaking in Prague, declared Czechoslovakia a **German protectorate**. Italy invades Albania. Russia occupies eastern Poland. On September 1**, Germany invades Poland.** Four weeks later, Germany and the USSR join in a **friendship treaty** and **divide Poland** between them. On <u>November 4</u>, the United States alters its Neutrality Act to permit the sale of weapons to European democracies.

<u>1940</u>   In <u>May</u>, **Germany invades France, Denmark, Norway**, **Belgium, the Netherlands** and **Luxembourg.** In <u>June,</u> **Italy** declares war on **France** and **Britain**. Vichy Government established in Occupied France, while Charles DeGaulle is recognized by the British as leader of the Free French. Estonia, Latvia, and Lithuania are incorporated into the USSR, and Alsace-Lorraine is incorporated into Germany in <u>August</u>. The military draft is instituted in the United States in August. Fifty American Destroyers are given to Britain in <u>September</u> in exchange for bases in British territory. **Tripartite Pact among Italy, Germany and Japan** is signed, also in September. **Italy attacks Greece** in <u>October</u>.

<u>1941</u>   **Germans invade Libya** in <u>February</u>. The Lend Lease Act is passed by U.S. Congress in <u>March,</u> and German ships in U.S. ports are seized. The USSR and Japan sign a neutrality pact in <u>April,</u> Yugoslavia falls to the Axis, and Greece surrenders. German warships withdraw from the Atlantic in <u>May</u>. U.S. freezes German and Italian assets in <u>June</u>, while the Germans, assisted by Romania, Finland, Hungary, Italy, Slovakia and Albania, invade the USSR. In <u>July</u>, the UK and USSR sign a mutual assistance agreement. On August 1, the **United States**

and Britain sign the Atlantic Charter, an eight-point declaration of human rights and war aims.** In <u>August</u>, British and Soviet forces join to occupy Persia, and on September 17 they reach Teheran, to discover that the day before Riza Pahlavi had abdicated his throne in favor of his son, Mohammed Riza Pahlavi. The German siege of Moscow begins in <u>October</u>, but by <u>December</u> they are in retreat before the Russians. In <u>October</u>, the **United States stops sending oil to Japan.** On <u>November 13</u>, the US Congress adopts President Roosevelt's amendments to the Neutrality Act. On <u>November 25</u>, Bulgaria, Denmark, Croatia, Finland, Romania, and Slovakia join the Anti-Comintern Pact. On <u>December 7</u>, the **Japanese attack Pearl Harbor**. On December 9, the puppet French government signs a treaty with Japan regarding Indo-China, and on the same day Free France declares war on Japan. During this month the **Japanese invade the Gilbert Islands, Guam, northern Borneo, Mindanao, Lingayen Bay, Wake Island, Hong Kong, and Sumatra.**

<u>1942</u>   In <u>January</u>, the **Japanese invade Burma** and the northern Solomon Islands. Rommel launches his last offensive in Libya. Thailand declares war on Britain and the United States. In <u>February</u>, the **Japanese capture Singapore** and Palembang (Sumatra). They invade Bali and Timor, and defeat an Allied naval force in the battle of Java Sea. In <u>March</u>, they capture Java and Rangoon (Burma), and land in New Guinea. The British retreat from the Andaman Islands. The one bright spot for the Allies is a **successful air attack on Japanese ships at Salamaua.** In the European theater, the RAF conducts a mass bombing of Lubeck, the British raid Saint-Nazare, and the Germans begin rounding up forced labor from occupied countries to free German workers for military service. In <u>April</u>, US ground forces on Bataan surrender, while our aircraft make their **first raid on Tokyo.** In <u>May</u>, the Japanese seize control of Mandalay, cutting off the Allied supply route to China through Burma. Admiral Nimitz's forces are **victorious** over the Japanese in the **Battle of the Coral Sea**. The British land on **Madagascar**. American forces on **Corregidor** and in **Mindanao** surrender. At **Auschwitz, Hitler commits his first multiple murder of Jews**. A **20-year mutual assistance pact is signed by the Soviets and the British**. The RAF sends its first 1,000-plane raid against Germany; Cologne is the target. In <u>June</u>, the United States **wins a decisive air and naval victory** over the Japanese at **Midway**. The Japanese land in the **Aleutians**, and the Germans launch a **general offensive against Russia**. In <u>July</u>, the **Allies** repulse Rommel at **El Alamein**, in **a decisive victory**. In <u>September</u>, the Germans reach **Stalingrad**, their **farthest penetration** into Russia. In <u>November</u>, **Montgomery** launches a successful offensive at **El Alamein**, while American and British forces land in **Morocco** and **Algeria**. The first French forces to resist the occupying Germans are organized. The US Marines win a decisive victory at **Guadalcanal.** The French fleet at Toulon is scuttled. In <u>December</u>, the **first atomic reaction is achieved** at a laboratory in Chicago.

<u>1943</u>   In <u>January</u>, Roosevelt and Churchill decide that they will accept **nothing short of unconditional surrender by both Germany and Japan**. In <u>February</u>, the Germans surrender at Stalingrad. British forces under Montgomery enter Tripoli. The Russians go on the offensive in the Ukraine, retaking Kharkov. The Japanese evacuate Guadalcanal. In <u>March</u>, Allied forces destroy a key Japanese convoy in the Bismarck Sea. The British Army breaches the Mareth Line, opening the way to Tunisia, where they are able to link up with the US First Army early in <u>April</u>. The remaining Axis forces in North Africa surrender on <u>May</u> 13. In <u>June</u>, Free French and Vichy French leaders join to free their country from German occupation. In <u>July</u>, **British and American forces land in Sicily.** The Allies bomb Rome for the first time. **Mussolini** is arrested, by order of **Victor Emmanuel III**, and replaced by **Marshal Pietro Badoglio**. In <u>August</u>, the Japanese occupiers of Burma declare its independence from the British Empire. **German resistance in Sicily is ended**, as the Allies capture Messina. In <u>September</u>, the **Italian army surrenders** to Allied Forces. The **Germans** respond by **occupying Italy** as far south as Rome. **Chiang Kai-shek** is elected **President of the Chinese Republic**. Allied forces establish bases in New Guinea. In <u>October,</u> Italy declares war on Germany, and Japan proclaims the independence of the Philippines (then an American colony). In <u>November</u>, the Germans "liberate" Kiev, the capital of the Ukraine. In late <u>November</u> and early <u>December</u>, **Churchill** and **Roosevelt** are in the Middle East, meeting separately with **Chiang Kai-shek, Stalin**, and **Ismet Inonu,** President of Turkey. France begins handing over power in Syria and Lebanon to native leaders.

<u>1944</u>   In <u>January</u>, Anglo-American forces **land at Anzio Beach**, in Italy. **Dwight Eisenhower** is appointed supreme commander of Allied Forces in Europe. US forces land on Marshall Islands. In <u>February</u>, the siege of Leningrad is lifted, and Novgorod liberated. Monte Cassino, a 1400-year-old Benedictine monastery, is bombed by the Allies. **Americans occupy Eniwetok**. In <u>March</u>, Berlin is raided in daylight for the first time. **Rome is bombed** on <u>March</u> 3, 10 and 14. US forces invade Hollandia, New Guinea. In <u>April</u>, Odessa and most of Crimea is liberated, with Sevastopol to follow early in <u>May.</u> In **Mid-May**, the **Allies** launch an **offensive up the Italian "boot"** toward Rome. <u>June</u> sees several major turning points. The **Allies** enter Rome on June 4, and two days later, on June 6, they **land on the Normandy beaches**. On the same day, there are uprisings against the occupying Germans in France, Belgium, Denmark and Norway. A week later, the Germans launch the **first V-bombs** against Britain. In <u>July</u>, an assassination attempt on Hitler fails, and Americans land on Guam. In <u>August</u>, the **people of Paris take control** of their city from the German occupiers, and there is a **national uprising in Slovakia**. In <u>September</u>, the **Allies enter Germany.** Hitler's response is to mobilize all males from 16 to 60 into a *Volkssturm*. In <u>October</u>, the **British land in Greece**, the Russians enter Hungary, East Prussia, and Czechoslovakia, and

the **Japanese fleet** is **defeated** at **Leyte**. In November, President **Roosevelt** is elected to an unprecedented **fourth term**. In December, the **Germans** launch their **final offensive** in the west, through Luxembourg into the **Ardennes** forest, aimed at southern Belgium. They are turned back by the end of the month.

1945   In January, the **American Sixth Army lands on Luzon** in the southern Philippines. The supply route to China through Burma is reopened. In February, American forces **liberate Manila**. At a **conference at Yalta**, Churchill, Roosevelt and Stalin agree on plans for the defeat of Germany. Allied forces cross the Rhine, and the **Russians liberate Budapest. Dresden**, known for its splendid architecture, is bombed into rubble. **US Marines land on Iwo Jima**. In March, Japanese forces on **Corregidor** surrender. **American forces cross the Rhine**. By the end of the month, the German army in the west has collapsed. The Yugoslav Republic is established, with Marshal Tito as president. Japan assumes power in Indochina. The Norwegian resistance undertakes a thousand acts of railroad sabotage. In April, US forces land on **Okinawa. Truman succeeds to the presidency**, on Roosevelt's death. Allied forces reach the Po River, in northern Italy. Member states of the United Nations meet in San Francisco to write its Charter. Italian partisans arrest Mussolini and execute him. **Hitler commits suicide** on April 30. In May, Berlin surrenders to the Soviet Army. Australians land on Borneo. Anglo-Indian forces drive the Japanese from Burma. **German forces surrender** *en masse* to Allied forces, or even to Resistance forces, as in Denmark, leading to unconditional surrenders throughout central Europe. In June, the **Supreme Allied Command assumes governing power in Germany.** The **United Nations Charter is signed**. In July, the liberation of the Philippines is completed. The **first experimental atomic bomb** is detonated, in New Mexico. American, Russian and British Heads of State meet at Potsdam to "settle the German problem." **Vietnam becomes an independent nation**. The British electorate votes Churchill out of office, and Clement Attlee succeeds him as Prime Minister. The Japanese government rejects an Allied ultimatum, leading in August to the **first use of atomic weapons**. In August, **Japan formally surrenders**, and is occupied by American forces. In September, **Ho Chi Minh** declares the independent **Republic of Vietnam**. In October, the **United Nations Charter** comes into effect. In November, war crimes trials are opened in Nuremberg, followed by similar trials in Tokyo, beginning in May 1946.

LIST OF VETERANS INTERVIEWED FOR THIS ORAL HISTORY

NAME	BRANCH OF SERVICE	CAMPAIGN	Page #
Barnett, Bob	Coast Guard	United States	169
Bass, Leon	Army	Battle of the Bulge	21
Blanche, John	Navy	*USS Missouri* Peace Treaty Tokyo Bay	190
Brossman, Howard	Army	Europe	24
Calabrese, Roy	Army AF (B-24)	Europe	29
Camilla, Joe	Army (medic)	Europe	31
Chesner, Pete	Army AF	China	97
Clappison, Charlie	Army	Okinawa	99
Clark, Arnett	Navy CBs	New Guinea	101
Clarke, Bill	Army AF (B-17) Stalag 17-POW escape	Europe Europe	32
Craighead, Bill	Navy	Pacific	103
Craighead, John and Frank	Navy	Pacific, Washington	107
Craighead, Sam	US Coast & Geodetic Survey	Alaska	171
Davis, Robert	Army	Europe	36
Dilks, Bob	Army	Pacific	111
Dishaw, Jack	Navy	Pacific	113
Donner, Ed	Merchant Marine	Europe & Pacific	40
Donovan, M. J.	Coast Guard	Atlantic	172
Emge, Ben	Navy Air Corps	Pacific	116
Errico, Bill	Navy	Pacific & Atlantic	118
Fager, Charles	Army AF	Europe	43
Fager Hummel	Navy	Pacific	120
Fullam, John	Navy	Pacific	122
Fulton, Chuck	Army	Europe	46
Fulton, June	Army Nurse Cadet	Stateside	175
Garner, Blaine	Army-Dr.	Europe	50
Gray, Sam	Army	Europe	52
Guenther, Fred	Army	Pacific-Tokyo	124
Hall, Glenn	Navy	Pacific	129
Hallowell, Tom	Research Chemist	Stateside	176
Hayman, Bill	Drug Researcher	Stateside	178
Hill, Bill	Army, MP	Europe	54
Hoegsted, Lou	Navy	Pacific-Atlantic	132

NAME	BRANCH OF SERVICE	CAMPAIGN	Page #
Hopkins, Don	Navy	Pacific-Atlantic	16
Jones, Parry	English CO	China	135
Kenderdine, Bob	Army	Pacific	137
Konicky, Walter	Army- POW	Pacific-Bataan	138
Kosan, Ernie	Army, Paratrooper	Europe	56
Kurtz, Jim	Marine, Communications	Pacific	142
Lancaster, Eileen	Army, Nurse	Stateside	180
Leedom, Vince	Navy, DE	Pacific	144
Mackey, Paul	Army, OSS	Europe	59
Mammel, Walt	Army	Europe-Pacific	64
Manahan, Ray	Navy, Doctor	Pacific	146
Matthews, Stan	Navy	Pacific	148
Miller, Richard	Army	Europe	66
Morrell, Pearl	Navy, WAVE	Washington, D.C.	182
O'Grady, Norman	Army	Europe	71
Olson, Bob	Navy	Pacific	150
Palmer, Creed	Army	Europe	74
Powell, Elizabeth	Navy, WAVE	Stateside	184
Rowell, Winston	Army	England	76
Rudolph, Robert (Kelly)	Army AF (B-17)	Europe	77
Smith, Harvey and Herbert	Army	Europe	78
Smith, Howard	Navy	Atlantic-Pacific	153
Smith, Jim	Army, General	Atlantic-Pacific	155
Stetson, Harold	Navy	Pacific	159
Stieber, George	Army AF (B-29)	Pacific	161
Streetz, John	Army	Stateside	187
Swayne, Kenneth	Army	Stateside	189
Swayne, Kingdon	Army	Europe Battle of Bulge	82
Swayne, Malcolm	Navy	Pacific	163
Turner, Joe	Army	Europe	86
Turpin, Ben	Army Cavalry	Europe	88
Wiggins, Clifton (Tip)	Navy	Atlantic-Pacific	164
Willis, Harry	Army – POW	Europe	92
Winn, Allan	Navy, Chaplain	Stateside & Pacific	166
Yamamoto, Al	Army AF	Europe	95

THEIR OWN STORIES

Authors, Kingdon W. Swayne and William M. Craighead at the World War II Memorial, Washington, D.C., June 8, 2005.

15

DON HOPKINS

December 7, 1941
Pearl Harbor

I was born in Princeton, Illinois on January 26, 1926. My mother and I lived in California, but I didn't like the schools. So in 1941, just before Pearl Harbor, I enlisted in the Navy as a 17-year-old with my parents' permission. The program was called "The skivvy cruise," requiring you to sign up for four years. After boot camp in San Diego, I spent nine weeks learning

Don Hopkins pointing to a picture of the USS Phoenix steaming out of Pearl Harbor after the attack.

how to do sheet metal work, to be a "striker," and then passed a test for submarine school. But instead of going to New London, I was sent to Pearl Harbor on an old tanker called the *Tippicanoe* because the Navy needed workers there. I then spent about a month on the *USS Richmond*, a World War I light cruiser, before I was transferred to the *Phoenix*, where I stayed for the rest of the war.

One Sunday morning in December 1941, I was standing down in my sleeping compartment. I was preparing for church services on the *Nevada*, putting on the dress uniform of white shorts, white T-shirt, and white hat. That's the last time I tried to go to church, because the Japanese suddenly began bombing the hell out of Pearl Harbor. I started up the ladder, but the Marines on top-side for colors almost ran me over trying to get down. When I did get up to look around, an ensign threw a machine gun over my shoulder, and told me to take it up to the superstructure. I ran up there with it, came back down, and reported to my battle station – the number two fire room. I stayed in the boiler room for 36 hours straight.

Within eight minutes, we had seven boilers on line and ready to get the hell out of there. We got around and started out on top-side. The gun crews were still at their battle stations. I could see only three of our ships: the *Phoenix, Honolulu*, and *St. Louis*, all light cruisers. There might have been some other ships in the distance, but I didn't look around that much, because I needed sleep. We then went looking for the Japanese fleet. Thank God we didn't find them; with their aircraft carriers, battleships and heavy cruisers, they would have kicked our butt all over the Pacific Ocean.

We stayed out in the ocean for 48 hours, cruising around at full speed so it would be harder for submarines to hit us. After we got back and refueled, we escorted two transports loaded with families of Navy personnel back to San Francisco. There, we replaced two of our anti-aircraft guns with two sets of pompom guns – the barrels of our anti-aircraft had gotten so hot during the fighting that the rifling in the barrels had slid out ten inches or so. Over the next month, we escorted ships from Pearl Harbor to San Francisco, and then picked up a big convoy – 15 to 20 ships – and headed for Australia. We went to Fremantle, on Australia's west coast, where we laid up for almost a month. We had to re-brick all the boilers, because we had burned them up at Pearl Harbor by going full right away, instead of warming the

VAdm. Kinkaid and Gen. MacArthur on board the USS Phoenix, February 1944.

The USS Phoenix steaming out of Pearl Harbor after the attack.

bricks up slowly. From Fremantle, we would go over to Perth, a city 11 miles away. I met a girl there and we set a time to get married. But we went on an escort and protect mission, and instead of returning to Fremantle, we kept right on going down the west coast past Melbourne, and up to Sydney.

From Australia, our ship went to the Philippine Islands

Don Hopkins with his granddaughter, Sarah Beth Marvel, in the memorabilia room.

-- Palandia and other places. We were trying to take the islands back from the Japanese. If our Navy hadn't gotten there when we did, the Japanese would have taken Australia, since they were not too far from Port Arthur at the time. When our ships converged, the Japanese didn't want to chance it.

We stayed up there for about three months, came back to Sydney for R&R and refueling and repairs, and then started back up to Georgian Islands. A leak around one of the shafts on the screws made us pull into Palandia, where they had a floating dry-dock. For the next year and a half, we went back and forth between Sydney and the Philippines. From there, we were sent back home to the Philadelphia Navy Yard for complete repairs. The Navy Yard wouldn't let Navy personnel do any work on the ship, so we had liberty 48-hour passes and 72-hour passes. We lived it up. And that's when I met my wife. Two other guys and I chased her and two cousins down a street in Philly, and finally caught up with them. I went with her a little over two weeks, and then got married. My mother had a conniption fit, saying she was just marrying me for my insurance, and everybody said it wasn't going to work. But they were all wrong – when my wife died in May 2003, we were just one month short of our 60th anniversary.

After all the repairs were done, we sailed from Philadelphia to Norfolk, and then down to San Juan. There, we picked up Cordell Hull, the Secretary of State, and took him to Casablanca for a big meeting in January 1943 with Roosevelt and Churchill. We dropped him off, turned around, and sailed through the Panama Canal back to the Philippines for two years.

The *Phoenix's* nickname was "the luckiest ship in the Navy." Although we were engaged in over 20 campaigns, including 12 major operations, we lost only three men out of our complement of 1100. One died from shrapnel wounds from a bomb, one committed suicide, and one fell overboard and we couldn't stop to find him. I feel I had the best gun crews in the Navy. For a little ship, we had plenty of guns: 15 main battery guns, all six inches; three 525 anti-aircraft guns on either side, and lots of 40 and 20 millimeters for anti-aircraft. Not many planes could get through the screen we laid down; we shot down two or three kamikazes and a lot of other planes. Our men earned a gold star and 11 bronze star medals.

We were called part of MacArthur's navy because he spent a lot of time on our ship. After the Battle of Leyte Gulf in October 1944, we took him to the island where he waded on shore and announced his return. Later, while we were refueling outside of Leyte Gulf, we got word that the Japanese fleet was headed back down to try and take the big island back. Halsey's fleet was way south trying to intercept the Japanese, but they weren't there. Instead, they were coming through the Surigao Straits. So we gathered our ships, including one battleship and a couple of heavy destroyers. The *Phoenix* was the flag ship for all the cruisers. We steamed up to the Surigao Straits, getting there long before the Japanese. When they came through, we nailed them. The battle began at 3:00 a.m. and lasted all night. It's every admiral's dream to cross the tee and we did it; we raced up and down each side of them. No airplanes were involved, just a ship-to-ship shoot-out. We sank a battleship, a couple of cruisers, and a whole bunch of destroyers. We lost only a couple of destroyers, plus lots of PT boats that were picked off like flies.

We were still in the Philippines when the war ended. The day the Japanese surrendered, our Captain gave the cooks all the liquor on the ship and had them make a big kettle of eggnog. Each man got a can of beer. Soon afterwards, they spun us around like a top and sent us home to the United States because we had a lot of leaks. At that point, we had been out at sea for a year and three months straight with no liquor except what the captain gave us, and no liberty; we were crazier than hell. When we pulled into San Pedro, California, they had a big party and show waiting for us.

Some of the guys who lived on the West Coast took leaves, so a skeleton crew brought the ship back to Philadelphia. I stayed on board because my wife was in Philly. I was what they called "main control" – I controlled the boilers from the forward engine room. When we pulled into Acapulco, Mexicans paddled out in canoes and sold us tequila and blackberry brandy. After we went through the Panama Canal, I was transferred to a World War I four-stacker destroyer that was being brought to Philadelphia for scrap. First day back in Philly, they gave me liberty, and I was reunited with my wife. I stayed on the *Phoenix* until she was decommissioned in 1946. Later, Argentina got the *Phoenix*, and the British sank her during the Falklands Island war.

After I was discharged, I stayed in Philadelphia. I had a variety of jobs – at Merck chemical plant as a boiler operator; in a "BB" (ballbreaker) plant running an old belt-driven cordless engine and firing the boilers too; at the Home for Incurables as an engineer; at J.E.Kunkel repairing oil burners; at Sun Shipbuilding in Chester; at Storywinn fuel company near Chester; and the Naval Ship Research and Development in Virginia. For seven years, I was sexton for a Catholic Church, taking charge of all the maintenance and the buying, including the communion wine.

After I retired in 1986, my wife and I lived near Wilmington, Delaware. My wife died in 2003 and is buried in the Delaware veteran's cemetery; when I go, I'll be put in the same vault with her. We had five children and now I'm living with a daughter in Chadds Ford, Pennsylvania. A great grandson was born on my birthday.

I have a lifetime membership with the Pearl Harbor Survivors' organization. Two thousand four hundred and three (2403) men died at Pearl Harbor. The *Phoenix* and I were both lucky.

LEON BASS

I was born in Philadelphia on January 23, 1925 and attended all-black schools until my junior and senior year in high school. In 1943, at the age of 18, I enlisted in the army, when I was living in Philadelphia. I was assigned to a number of army posts in the south, where I was subject to discrimination on buses, in restaurants, and in bathrooms. In the fall of 1944 my unit was sent to Europe. After about two months in a small English town called Fording Bridge, we sailed to LeHavre, arriving about Christmas time. We were assigned to a small town in Belgium called Martelange, where our task

Leon Bass

was to rebuild a bridge to serve the Allied forces whose mission was to relieve the men of the 101st Airborne Division who were at Bastogne, surrounded by German forces. The bridge did the job. It was a glorious day in my life, a wonderful experience.

But that feeling was short-lived. My next experience was watching graves registration trucks pass by, loaded with corpses of American soldiers. I asked myself why I had enlisted in the military service of the nation that treated me as a second-class citizen.

As the war went on, we passed through France, Belgium, and Luxembourg, and then crossed the Rhine into Germany, passing through Frankfurt, Cologne, Dusseldorf, Bad-Kreuznach, Eisenach, and finally Nuremberg. At Weimar, we found ourselves in the Buchenwald concentration camp. There I met the "walking dead." Human beings reduced to skin and bone from starvation and torture. I met a Polish prisoner who spoke English. He told us that the inmates were Jews, gypsies, Jehovah's Witnesses, Catholics, trade unionists, communists, and homosexuals. He also directed me to another building, where the German doctors had placed jars of body parts, including eyes, ears, hearts, livers and kidneys, genitals, and fingers. There was a lampshade made of human skin, chosen because it had been tattooed. As I moved on, I passed several dying children. Next I reached the crematorium, with stacks of dead bodies outside. Inside there were six ovens. I was told that the ashes were taken to farms for use as fertilizer. My reaction to this experience was a determination to do something about racism and bigotry when I got home.

At the end of the war in Europe I was reassigned to the Philippines, and then returned home to Philadelphia. My parents had hoped to send me to college, but we didn't have the money. The GI Bill of Rights made it possible for me to go to college, and I applied to West Chester State College, and was accepted. But I found that I could not live in the dorm, and when I went to the movies in town I was told to sit in the balcony. But I walked right past the usher, sat on the main floor, and was not thrown out. Later, as I walked back to my room, I thought I was ten feet tall. It was the most difficult situation I had ever faced, and I had triumphed.

I graduated from college in 1949, and got a job teaching in an all-black elementary school in Philadelphia, where I had 29 youngsters in my class, to whom I taught basic skills, reading, spelling, social studies and science. But it was clear to me that what they really needed was hope, which I could not deliver.

About that time a black woman, Rosa Parks, who lived in Montgomery, Alabama, refused to move to the back of the bus. She was jailed. Her friends responded by refusing to use buses. For thirteen months they walked. The Montgomery bus boycott was the beginning of the civil rights movement in the United States. The Supreme Court declared the segregated buses to be unconstitutional. Martin Luther King urged the black people of Montgomery to take their rightful places on the buses "with dignity, and with love in your hearts." I found this hard to understand, but it worked.

Shortly thereafter, Dr. King came to Philadelphia and spoke at a playground on Birch Street near Temple University, and near my school. I took my students there to hear him. He was small in stature but he was a giant of a man. He spoke of loving, of nurturing, of compassion and understanding, of respecting all people. He told them that even if their life work was sweeping the streets, they should sweep the streets like Beethoven wrote the music, like Michelangelo painted his pictures, like Shakespeare wrote his poetry. Whatever you do, be the best. I was mesmerized. No one ever touched me that way before. I went back to my school, determined to do more.

When I learned, in 1963, that Dr. King would be appearing in Washington, I went down to join 250,000 others on the Mall, where we heard Dr. King say his now famous words, "I have a dream that one day people will be judged not by the color of their skin, but by the content of their character." I was with rich people, poor people, black people, white people, Jews, Gentiles, Catholics, Protestants, and all kinds of people, crying unashamedly.

Back in Philadelphia, I served as principal of an elementary school. In 1968, the superintendent asked me to move up to Benjamin Franklin High School, the toughest school in the city, and maybe in the whole country. I agreed to do it. The first day I went to work there, I was accosted by a group of young toughs, demanding to know what changes I would bring to the school. When I told them to give me some time to get organized, I was told, "mister, if you don't do something right away, we gonna burn this place down."

It was tough. I walked around the school for a couple of months with a dull headache. I tried to bring order out of chaos, to persuade the boys that education was the most important thing for them. But I couldn't get a handle on it, until one day I passed a classroom where a woman visitor from Europe named Nina Koleska was describing her experience at Auschwitz, one of the worst concentration camps in Europe. They were rude, and not listening. I told them I had been there, and knew that what she was telling them was true. They got quiet. She told them about the loss of her parents, grandparents, three brothers and a sister, all victims of the gas chambers and those despicable ovens that turned them into fertilizer. They shook her hand and then walked out of the classroom in silence, something I had never seen before. We talked afterward, and she convinced me that I should share with others my experience of Buchenwald. That was in 1976. I have been talking ever since.

HOWARD BROSSMAN

I was born on January 29, 1915 in Womelsdorf, Pennsylvania, and moved to Rehrersburg when I was in third grade. I lived and worked on a farm there for the rest of my life.

In 1942, I was working for the Narrow Fabric Company. We made parachute cord for the military parachutes. I was drafted in June, and was sent to Harrisburg for a physical, with the understanding that we would be sent home for two weeks to settle our affairs and then report for duty. I was sent instead directly to Camp Meade, Maryland. We arrived about midnight, and at 4:00 AM I was tapped on the feet and told to get up and report to KP. In the

Howard Brossman

meantime, the other recruits were told they could go home and report back in two weeks. It wasn't until nine months later that I was able to visit my family.

From Camp Meade I was assigned to Camp Pickett in Virginia, where new barracks had just been built, and all we did was clean windows. At first we didn't even have rifles, so they gave us each a rifle-sized piece of wood to carry during drills. Soon thereafter, we were issued rifles. They were packed in cosmoline, a greasy rust preventive. It took us days to get the rifles clean.

I spent the next six months in Camp Blanding, Florida. It was hot when we arrived, and it was tough, drilling and crawling around in the sand. But by the time we left, it seemed really cold, especially when walking guard at night along the railroad tracks. From Camp Blanding we went up to Camp Rucker, Alabama for maneuvers, and then back to Blanding. Our next stop was Camp Forrest, Tennessee.

After a couple of months we moved to Camp Laguna, Arizona. The temperature reached as high as 115°, but the air was dry, so it was no worse than 90° here. One Sunday, a group of about 50 of us went to the Grand Canyon, where we swam across the Colorado River. We ended up a couple of blocks downstream. The worst thing about Camp Laguna was the sand storms. You felt like the skin of your face was being cooked.

My next assignment was in Kansas, at a camp whose name I have forgotten. It was close to Wichita, where they made the B-29 bombers. One day, we watched the sky fill up with those planes. I've never seen anything like it. In the age of atomic bombs, we will never see a sky full of planes again.

Our next stop was Camp Miles Standish, in Boston. From there, in April 1944 we were shipped out to Europe. Ours was the last ship in the convoy, the one most vulnerable to torpedoes. Every once in a while you could hear the "boom, boom" of depth charges from the destroyers.

We arrived safely at the Firth of Clyde, in Scotland. But our base was in England, from which we once went on maneuvers in Wales.

Two or three days after D-Day, we entered Normandy over the beaches, landing in the evening at high tide, then waiting until morning, when the tide was out, and we were in only about two feet of water. We lowered the bow doors and landed our heavy equipment. As soon as the doors opened, we were strafed by the Luftwaffe. I ran up the beach and under some trees, whose leaves and twigs came down like confetti, in what turned out to be a very brief strafing that didn't do any damage.

In an apple orchard, we awaited the arrival of the rest of the division. One of our guys left his pup tent just before the German planes arrived, leaving his rifle behind. When he returned, he found that the stock of the rifle had been destroyed by a German bullet. Next we were strafed by our own P-38's! Our captain pulled the camouflage off one of our trucks so our pilots could see the star. That did the trick.

Our next mission was to take control of the port of Cherbourg, to give our forces a deep-water port in France. On the way up the Cotentin Peninsula, we had to cope with hedgerows. These consist of small trees and shrubs growing from earthen banks 6-8 feet high, which separate one field from another. In many of the corners, there were machine guns left by the Germans. The area was also mined. We successfully coped with both mines and hedgerows by putting a bulldozer blade on the front of each tank. We knew the hedgerows were man-made, so we knew men could unmake them. Shelling from our artillery led to the surrender of 400 German officers and 2,000 soldiers.

We then turned to the south, back down the same peninsula, to La Haye du Puis. Farther on, there was a river which we crossed on pontoon bridges. We were worried that the Germans might blow up the bridge, but they didn't. We crossed successfully. Our fears that the Germans might make a serious effort to push us back again were laid to rest when our anti-aircraft guns and our Air Force downed 14 German planes.

Our mission was to take Paris, but the Germans had already left by the time we arrived. Hitler had ordered the destruction of Paris, but the German general on the spot had a little more sense. He just left. Fortunately for him, they lost the war. The patch on our shoulder identified us as the "Cross of Lorraine Division," which led to choosing us, initially, to liberate Paris. But in the end, the honor was given to a Free French division. All I saw of Paris was the top of the Eiffel Tower, from a distance. We moved on east, through France.

At Christmas time in 1944 we were headed for the German border, when General Patton ordered our division to move north to Belgium and Holland. We passed through Metz on the way. In the town of Hagenau, near the German border, we came under artillery fire. The buildings on both sides of the street were burning, but none of us were hit. There was new snow on the ground, and the road got icy. Our general ordered us to get out promptly. Our tank treads just slipped on the ice, so we put chains on a four-wheel-drive ammunition truck and pulled the tank along.

We got to Belgium and Holland successfully, but the cold was terrible. We didn't have overshoes, our feet were wet, and our clothing frozen to our bodies. The Dutch people were very kind to us, inviting us to sleep in their houses. They put us up in their bedrooms and kitchens while they slept in the cellars. They might also have felt safer in the cellars, in fear both of German bombing, and of Allied planes misjudging the location of their target at Aachen. My host family were the Jungens and their 17-year-old son, Willie. I corresponded with this family after the war.

Before we could pass through Aachen on our way east, bulldozers had to clear the road of debris from our bombings.

Essen, about 30 miles further into Germany, was our next destination. We did a lot of shooting there. Passing us heading west were Germans who had surrendered. In Essen we set up our guns near the Krupp ammunition works. We became aware of a young German general, in his late 30's, one of Hitler's favorites, who declared that American soldiers were "a bunch of choir boys."

I don't remember the name of the next town we passed through, but I recall that it was the site of a supply depot. We did a lot of shooting there. We were headed toward the Ruhr River.

I was an artillery gunner, firing 155-millimeter Howitzers. We were part of an army corps, whose name I don't remember. We accepted the surrender of a German general, whose one request was that he not be turned over to the French. We never knew why.

On another occasion, in France, our artillery managed, by mistake, to get out in front of our infantry. We met some French people, who tried to tell us something, but we couldn't understand them. They were trying, I think, to warn us of the approach of some German planes. Our lieutenant and I found shelter under the roots of a large tree. The planes returned several times and put out of action our jeep and weapons carriers. Our bags and bedrolls were on one of the jeeps, looking like they had been chewed by rats. But it could have been worse. If the French hadn't warned us, we probably would have driven right into a trap.

On our way to the Ruhr River we passed through Gelsenkirchen, Reneshaffen, and another town. We stopped short of the Rhine, joining in the bombardment of German troops on the east side with 155-mm Long Toms and 240s. I remember being told to "fire at will," and hearing our guys ask, "Who the hell is Will?"

We crossed the Rhine on a pontoon bridge, to find that the Germans had retreated eastward. I don't remember the names of the towns we passed through. But I remember one incident when we were getting our guns into position. Two Germans appeared in front of us, saying, "Achtung. Nicht schiessen," meaning "Attention, don't shoot." I said to them, "Achtung. Hand der Hohe," meaning "Attention, Hands up high." They came down to us and we took them prisoner and sent them to the rear.

I can remember stopping at Dortmund. We were not too far from Berlin, and the Allies had promised the Russians that they could take Berlin. That was fine with me, because the fighting there was fierce. We heard that two Russian divisions were fighting each other. One had approached from the north and the other from the south. But when the Russians entered Berlin, they were greeted by German kids throwing Molotov cocktails (a crude incendiary grenade, named after the Russian statesman).

We passed through Stuttgart on our way to Berlin. I talked after the war to a friend then living about 20 miles from Stuttgart, who remembered being able to read a newspaper at night by the light of the burning city. When the Germans surrendered, we were at Dortmund, not too far from Berlin. We stopped, by Allied agreement, to permit the Russians to take Berlin. We became part of the Army of Occupation. We took control of a German Air Force camp of 90,000 prisoners of war. Our first task was to help transport German soldiers to their hometowns. I should have been riding in a jeep, but I discovered it was warmer in a Volkswagen with a few prisoners. They would ask me for things, and I would do my best to respond.

I married Lizzie Zeller in Stouchsburg, Pennsylvania on August 28, 1948. We have seven children, the first born in 1950 and the last in 1962. The children in the order they were born are Dolores, Paul, Allen, Clarence, Sarah, Carl, and Kathy. At present there are 15 grandchildren and 7 great grandchildren.

Compiler's Note:
(As recalled by Howard's daughter, Dolores)
This friendship between the Jungen and Brossman families continued for years after the war with an exchange of letters and telephone conversations in the hopes that sometime the families would meet. It wasn't until June of 1996 that Willie and his wife, Annie, came to visit Howard and his wife, Lizzie, on their farm in Rehrersburg, Pennsylvania. At that time, they stayed for a week. The second visit was in 1998 when both Willie and Annie came to visit, again for a week.

(As recalled by Howard's daughter, Sarah)

I went to Europe to see the Jungens in 2000 with my niece, Sarah, and again in 2002 with my brother Carl and his daughter, Destiny. It was a memorable visit and we heard wonderful stories of Daddy and what it was like being there during WWII. In 2004, I finally convinced my Mom, Lizzie, to make the trip. On this trip we went into the house where Daddy stayed during combat. It had been modernized, but Willie told us what it looked like during the war. It was interesting listening to the stories that Willie told. We went to the American cemetery and drove around the countryside.

ROY CALABRESE

I was born January 27, 1920 in Calabria, at the "toe" of Italy's "boot." My last name comes from the name of the town. When I was four, our family moved to Hazelton, and later to Tamaqua, Pennsylvania. After graduating from high school there, I went into the military.

I enlisted in the Air Force in January 1942, and had six months' training as an Air Force mechanic in Mississippi. I was then assigned to a factory in Baltimore where the B-26 Marauder bomber was made; I got thoroughly acquainted with it.

In April 1943 I was flown in a B-17 bomber to England, where we stayed 18 months. From then until the end of the war I was stationed in France, at about six different bases. I worked on the propel-

Roy Calabrese

lers and hydraulic systems of B-26 bombers. They flew at medium altitude, were much faster than the B-17s, and carried a nine-man crew.

I didn't fly on any combat missions, only test hops after we installed a new engine or propeller. The squadron we supported had the least losses in the group.

At the end of the war, I was briefly in Germany. I returned home in October 1945 on the *Aquitania,* a passenger liner commandeered for troop use in wartime, and was discharged at Indiantown Gap Pennsylvania. I received $20 a week for up to 52 weeks, or until I found a job.

I returned home to Tamaqua, where I got a job in a bakery. I was also in the Civilian Conservation Corps in the 1940s. I was stationed in Columbus, New Mexico, where we repaired roads and built dams.

I was in the Air Force reserves, so I was called up in January 1952 for the Korean War. I did shop maintenance on aircraft in New Jersey, and was discharged in December 1952.

In February 1953 I got married to Irene, who lived in Lansford, near Tamaqua. I was working at the Middletown Airport near Harrisburg. But I was laid off in 1954, so I came to live in Newtown and found a job at Kaiser Aircraft in Trenton. Kaiser was taken over by Strukoff, and I worked for them for a year. I took the civil service exam for work in the post office, and also went to Beauty School, where I got a beautician's license. That was my wife's suggestion. She worked in a beauty shop, and I joined her there for three years.

In 1962 I was employed by the post office in Newtown, and remained there for 28 years, until 1990. When I retired from the post office, I received credit toward my pension for my seven years' service in the reserves.

JOE CAMILLA

I was born in the village of Holland, Pennsylvania on February 28, 1914. When the United States entered World War II, I was living on Penn Street in Newtown. I had quit school when I was 14, and went to work at 35 cents an hour, 11 hours a day, in a wallpaper factory in Penndel. I had married Rosanna Bohmler in 1939, and by 1944, when I was drafted at the age of 30, I had two daughters. After the war we had a third. A month after I was drafted, they stopped taking fathers. I was inducted at the New Cumberland Army Depot. My next stop was Abilene, Texas, where I spent six months in training as a medic. In October 1944 I crossed the Atlantic to Liverpool in a converted ocean liner that carried 7,000 men. We immediately took a train to Southampton, where we crossed the English Channel.

Joe Camilla

I was assigned to a camp for about 400 German prisoners in Normandy where I remained until the end of the war. Most of my time in Europe I spent as an army medic. While there I learned that as an adolescent I had had tuberculosis, which had been cured, miraculously, without medical intervention. I

Joe Camilla and Congressman Fitzpatrick

came home in February 1946, and was discharged at New Cumberland.

Before the war I had made some money as a prizefighter, with 43 fights in about five years. I received only one cut eye, well below the average. I knocked out 18 opponents. I won most of the other fights, though I lost a few.

Harry Shields, then the Mayor of Newtown, asked me if I would like to be a part-time cop. I worked part-time for nine years, then signed on full time. I have also been active in the Exchange Club. I still live in Newtown, at the Friends Home for the past two years. The food is good, and nice people run it. I enjoy being of assistance to fellow residents who are less able.

BILL CLARKE

I served in the Air Force for 32 years. In the fall of 1941 I had been working for a year and a half at Brewster Aeronautics Corporation in Johnsville, Pennsylvania, as a mechanic on the flight-line and engine-line. On Pearl Harbor Day, I broke my nose while playing football in Distan Ball Park on State Road in Tacony. As a critical defense worker, I was not subject to the draft. But the next day three of us, Tony Margione, Bill Andressi (my brother-in-law) and I went downtown to join the Navy. Tony was rejected because he was an inch too short.

Bill Clarke and his wife.

My brother-in-law, a carpenter, was assigned to the Seabees. I went up to New Cumberland, Pennsylvania, where I was assigned to the Air Corps and sent to Miami Beach for basic training and then to Sheppard Field in Texas for engineering school. From there I went to Tindall Field in Florida for gunnery training. I was reclassified as an engineer-gunner, and sent to Daybar Park, Florida. Though I had been trained on medium bombers, I was assigned to a B-17, a four-engine plane that was our largest at the time, with a crew of ten.

After a period of flying coast patrol to seek out German submarines, I was assigned to England. We were supposed to go there via the southern route through South America to Marrakesh, but when we arrived there we learned that the B-17s had several faulty pieces of equipment that had to be replaced. So we were shipped back home on C-54s to Hunter Field in Savannah, Georgia, where the replacement equipment was installed. We then left the planes there, took a train to Camp Kilmer, New Jersey, stayed overnight, and the next morning boarded the *Queen Elizabeth*. Five and a half days later, we were in Scotland. I don't know why we didn't fly our own planes over. That was the normal practice.

A fellow passenger on the *Queen Elizabeth* was Joe Lewis, a buck sergeant at the time. I have always admired him. I remember him, when champion of the world, fighting at a fund-raiser for Army-Navy Relief. His wife and his managers got all his money, and he died a poor man. Mohammad Ali, by contrast, declared that he was a Muslim priest and a conscientious objector, so he avoided military service. In the same way, Mickey Mantle avoided military service by claiming two bad knees, yet he could run around the bases for years.

We were already assigned to a crew when we sailed for England, along with 71 other bombardment crews and a battalion or so of soldiers, ten to fifteen thousand in all. The swimming pool had been turned into a mess hall. We could eat whenever we wanted, but there was a pass system to keep us from going back a second time. Anti-aircraft protection for the ship was provided by American GIs during the day and by the British at night. Our ship was so fast that it didn't need escorts, nor did it follow a zigzag route. On the fantail, we had a view of the enormous screw that was propelling us through the water. On the bow, we could observe the 40-foot waves that the ship was plowing through.

We wound up in Greenock, Scotland, and were greeted by a parade of soldiers in kilts. We immediately boarded a train for England, stopped overnight at Duncan Hall and Bede Hall. The next day we arrived at our base in southern England, at a little town in Suffolk called Rattleston, right outside of Ipswich. I was in the 447th Bomb Group, 710th Bomb Squadron. All my 13 missions took us into Germany, many of them to the V1 and V2 sites from which rockets were being fired at London. We bombed Berlin three times, losing 60 or more bombers each time. Our 8th Air Force lost more men, 45,000, than the entire US Navy.

I remember taking off in the fog, and flying through solid overcast until we reached about 15,000 feet. It was a miracle that we didn't run into each other. All our flights were during the day. The British flew at night. When we were returning to Britain we used IFF (Identification: Friend or Foe) to tell the British anti-aircraft gunners who we were.

The day we went down, our mission was to bomb a half-mile area within which Hitler was supposed to be having a meeting, which we had learned was scheduled to start at 11:56 AM. The 385th Squadron was part of our wing, and was leading the attack, commanded by Frank Volesh, and guided by a radar we called the Mickey Set. Volesh had lost seven B-17s, but never lost a crew member. This time we were getting the shit shot out of us. Now the fighters jumped us.

We lost ten planes near Magdeburg, all shot down by German aircraft. Our navigators were pretty good at finding their way through anti-aircraft fire. But it was tougher when the Germans put their anti-aircraft guns on trains and hid them in tunnels, from which they suddenly emerged when we flew over.

The plane that I was on when we were shot down was one I had tried to avoid being assigned to, because it was pretty well beat up. On my last flight we lost two engines, and also discovered that the landing gear had been ignited by a malfunctioning engine. Three times I lowered the landing gear, hoping that the fire would be blown out. Fortunately, the entire crew survived the crash, though we had abandoned the plane at 27,000 feet, and had no oxygen until we had dropped to 17-18,000 feet. Our tail gunner was shot through the throat, where a tourniquet was impossible, so we tightened a towel around his neck. He got to the ground safely, was picked up by the Germans, and today is alive and living in Connecticut.

For thirteen months, I was a prisoner of war at Stalag 17, in Krems, Austria. Our book, put together by our camp leaders, tells the whole story: the names of the German officers, the war crimes, the camp leaders, the medics, the priest, everybody. It was a great group to be a part of, for any needed skill was there.

If you wanted to escape, you went to the escape committee, which would equip you with food, clothing, and a compass. They would judge the likelihood of your success and the risk of harm to others. Very few plans were approved.

I managed to escape, while we were on a forced march. By this time, the Germans had retreated in the face of the Russian invasion. Russian officers entered the prison camp under a white flag, told the Germans that Russian forces would soon take over the camp, and that if any Allied prisoners were hurt in the process, German officers would be held for war crimes.

So in the middle of the night, we were marched in groups of 500 to 800 all the way from Krems to Brunau, at the confluence of the Inns and Salzach Rivers. It was one hell of an ordeal, without food, or winter clothing. We stopped for the night in a forest. We tried to make shelters, but without tools, we were limited to whatever branches we could break off with our hands. We asked for water, and the Germans told us to melt snow. We refused, and found our way to the river bank, where we had only cupped hands as drinking vessels. With me at the river bank were my waist-gunner friend Ken Curry, and a Philadelphian named Walt Zimmerman. He was far stronger than I. He had a lot of D-bars stored in his coat, and never gave one to a fellow Philadelphian. But in the end, I was the only one from this area to attend Zimmerman's funeral in Florida, just a couple of months ago. Zimmerman's excuse for disappointing me was that he had to take care of Fred Inman and Vince Pale. The latter was badly burned, he said, and nearly frozen.

The moment our guard turned his back to light a pipe or cigarette, I jumped into the river. It was April, but the river was fed from melting snow fields, so the water was very cold. Sometimes I could catch a ride on a floating log, and gradually made my way to the other side, where I lay all day. As I approached some troops, not knowing whether they were Russians or Americans, the first words I heard were "You rotten son of a bitch!"

I walked right up to them, for they had no sentries posted, which was pretty stupid. I could have been a Kraut. They were building a pontoon bridge across the river, to replace one blown up by the Krauts. The top-ranking person there was an NCO named Bill McCarthy. I urged them not to fire across the river, because there was a prison camp there with 4,500 of our guys. I also urged them to get some food to those guys. Later the Russians mortared the camp and overran it, not knowing it contained Allied prisoners.

McCarthy was suspicious of me, fearing that I might be a German spy. While

I was wearing GI pants, I was also wearing a German flying jacket and German officers' boots. He was finally reassured when I was able to answer his questions about the Yankee catcher (Bill Dickey) and about Dagwood and Blondie.

I am the one who brought back the 13th Armored to liberate Stalag 17, which contained 4,100 fliers. Bill McCarthy was the name of the first sergeant. I have attended some of their reunions.

When I was interrogated by the Germans, they put me in a sweat box, but most of what they wanted to know, I couldn't have told them. As we were supposed to do, I gave them only my name, rank and serial number. They responded by telling me where I had lived, my father's job, where I went to school, and the name of the carrier in the Pacific where my brother was serving. They could have done the same thing for anyone else in the 8th Air Force.

In the prison camp, I tried to be as inconspicuous as possible, so I wouldn't be missed if I escaped. The German prison guards would salute us with "Heil Hitler," and require that we salute back. You got your ass kicked if you didn't do it. At first we had roll calls every half hour around the clock.

Our guards were probably nice guys before the war, but by now some would have had their whole families wiped out by our bombing.

We never got meat, and there was no gravy. The bread was 40% sawdust. You never heard such farts in your life. We called them "flak."

We learned to make a barley soup that was like oatmeal, to which we added raisins from our Red Cross packages. The packages also contained some oleo-margarine. Since there was no bread to spread it on, we would put a wick in the oleo and burn it as a candle.

The US government paid me $2.50 for every day I was a prisoner, drawn from German assets confiscated in the United States. What was left over was returned to the Germans by Attorney General Bobby Kennedy.

In 1998, I was chosen to be the #1 POW, which meant that my wife and I were flown to England at the expense of the Air Force. We went to Suffolk to a top secret base, for the Gulf War was going on. But all I did was stand retreats and participate in wreath-laying ceremonies.

Compiler's Note:

In Clarke's home there is a plaque reading:

"Special Recognition to Top Sergeant William Clarke. We, the members of Stalag 17 prisoners of war take this occasion to honor you for your assistance at the time of our release. Swimming across the cold Inns River in Austria during the middle of the night, you met soldiers building a pontoon bridge across the river and informed them of our presence. This is a long overdue thank you." (Signed) Jake Stein, May 8, 1997 reunion at Tucson, Arizona.

ROBERT DAVIS

I was born on January 1, 1920, and raised in Law-renceville, New Jersey. I went to the public elementary school, and then to Lawrenceville Prep School, graduating in 1938.

In 1942 I graduated from Princeton, where I had also served as a leader in a 250-man ROTC artillery unit. After attending several artillery refresher courses in the summer of 1942, I was assigned in the fall to an artillery battalion of the 13th Army Division then stationed at Camp Ville CA. Our weapons were 105mm howitzers mounted on medium tanks minus their tops. We had a total of eighteen 105s. By the fall of 1943, I was a first lieutenant and a battery commander, a great job.

Bob Davis (left) and his tank crew.

But in the summer of 1944, right after the Normandy invasion, I stupidly volunteered to go to Europe as a replacement. In my new unit I didn't know anyone, and was the low man on the totem pole. I was no longer a battery commander, but a mere forward observer, in command of a tank and relaying requests for artillery fire back to the battery commanders. We crossed the English Channel from Southampton and landed on Utah Beach at a time when the front line was about 20 miles inland. We first encountered the Germans at Chartres, where our orders required us not to fire at the cathedral.

We crossed the Moselle River, with Metz as our destination. As we paused on the way, a supply truck arrived with rations and water. We knew the Germans were nearby. I also knew we needed food and water. When a supply truck arrived with a delivery, I told two of my men to bring the supplies from the truck. When they balked, I went after the supplies myself, and was struck by a nasty looking piece of shrapnel, which went right across my back and dug itself in. I was sent to a recuperation hospital. There were towns within walking distance, so we would go to one, get a bottle of wine, and sit down on the sidewalk to enjoy the beautiful fall foliage.

I was soon able to return to my unit, now in Holland. Toward the end of November, we moved to the German-Dutch border, just north of Belgium. Our mission was to gain control of the dams on the Roer River, so the Germans would be unable to release the dammed waters and deny the Allies the ability to cross the river.

On December 17, about 2:00 AM, we received orders to move out. I can still remember the cursing that accompanied our efforts to find our belongings and get them properly packed. What we didn't realize was that we were right in the path of the "Bulge," the familiar name for the Germans' last-ditch effort to break through Luxembourg and Belgium to the English Channel, dividing the Americans from the British and surrounding the latter. We were not far from the site of the Malmedy massacre, where the First SS Panzer Division surprised and killed most of the members of an American unit whose main job was to locate German artillery forces so our troops could fire on them. We were on the road all night, headed for a site north of St. Vith. We remained there until December 21, when the Germans attacked from the south. We pulled back to a point about four miles west of St. Vith, bypassing the town of Rodt, which the Germans had occupied. We abandoned the roads and drove through the fields, knocking down fences.

It was so foggy that we couldn't direct our artillery properly. They had to calculate their aim by using map coordinates. As for me, I earned that day my second Purple Heart, but it was awarded for superficial burns from white phosphorus shells. I remained at my post.

Our division commander, General Hasbrook, persuaded General Montgomery, the British commander of our area, that our 7th Armored Division must be pulled out if we were to be of future use. We pulled back through the 82nd Armored Division which had set up a line of defense along a railroad track at Poteau, to a little Belgian town called Manhay. That is where I got my first night's sleep in a week, in my bedroll in the hay in a farmer's barn. That was wonderful!

The Germans attacked the next morning. Our Colonel sent my crew out

Bob Davis and John Eisenhower

with Lt. McNamara, ordering me to stay behind because I had "been up for a week." Their tank was knocked out by German fire, but the crew returned safely. All my gear was in that tank.

I was assigned, as a forward observer, to an infantry unit whose position overlooked Manhay. Whenever I saw action in the town I would call the artillery. After a couple of days of that, I rejoined an armored unit.

Let me describe briefly the tanks we used. The Wright Continental had an aircraft engine that was incredibly noisy; it had to be gunned when you turned a corner. My second tank was a diesel, with a good motor. My last one was a Sherman tank with a Ford engine; and it was beautiful. It weighed about 30 tons, and was equipped with a 75-millimeter main gun, a 50-caliber machine gun and two 30-caliber machine guns.

The regular German tanks, the Panzers, had long-barrel 76-millimeter guns. They also had some 60-ton monsters, The Tigers, with an 88-millimeter gun that could be used against tanks, personnel, or aircraft. Their tanks and ours had about the same top speed: 25-30 miles an hour.

During the encounter in St. Vith, I had worked closely with General Bruce Clarke as his forward observer. He asked me to join his staff, so I spent the rest of the war as his Assistant S-3 (Operations Officer) Air, with the mission of calling in air support to attack enemy forces as we engaged them. General Clarke later commanded the 1st Armored Division, and went on to head up all the American forces in Europe. I remained with General Clarke until the end of the war.

By February 1945 we were on the move again, and I was promoted to Captain. Our unit crossed the Roer at Remagen, on a pontoon bridge, and moved across Germany to the Elbe River, about 40 miles from Berlin. The last maneuver was led by a brilliant West Pointer, Lt. Bill Knowlton, who later was the Commandant at West Point, and retired as a four-star general.

At the Elbe we met the Russians. I remember joining them in toasting Roosevelt, Stalin, and Studebaker, the latter because we had sent the Russians a fleet of Studebaker trucks.

I was discharged from the Army in October 1945, and the following year I married Dorothy Nightingale. We went to live in Wyoming, on a ranch on the North Platte River owned by a cousin. We took charge of a camp for fishermen, mostly from Denver, with the help of a hired cook and maid. We also fed the ranch workers, whom I sometimes helped in haying season. A few months of that was enough, so we returned to Lawrenceville, where we found a rent-free cottage owned by a friend of my mother. I went to Rutgers for a short course in agriculture, and the next spring—1954, I think—we bought a small farm between Allentown and New Egypt, New Jersey.

A year on the farm was enough for us. In October 1955 we bought the Newtown Hardware House, which we operated for the next thirty years. In 1990 I sold it to Dave Callahan, who still runs it. I have been active in the Newtown Baptist

Church, where I have taught the men's class for about 30 years. I was president of the Council Rock PTA for a year, and also president of the Newtown Rotary Club, an organization I enjoyed very much.

In retirement, I still fish, hunt, and garden. Our next move, in the future, will be to sell our house and move into Pennswood Village retirement community.

Not so long ago Bob Kenderdine, a Newtown friend, and I took a trip to visit the Battle of the Bulge area. We spent several days in Malmedy, then went to St. Vith. We found many foxholes still there. Let me remind you briefly of the Battle of the Bulge. Hitler's plan was to cross the Meuse River and move rapidly to Antwerp, the Allies' main supply base. The Germans attacked with two Panzer armies and one of infantry, a total of about 20 divisions. Their front was about 60 miles wide, and they penetrated our lines about 50 miles. They never reached the Meuse. A number of years ago, the German and American commanding generals met to critique the battle. When General Clarke asked General Mantuffel why he had failed to surround and eliminate a vulnerable American unit, Mantuffel replied that Hitler's orders were to proceed straight ahead, toward Antwerp.

Allied casualties in the Bulge were 20,000 killed and 80,000 wounded. German casualties were 30,000 killed and 70,000 wounded.

Ed Donner

I was born in Palmerton, Pennsylvania on October 11, 1922, and graduated from Palmerton High School. I was active in the Boy Scouts, achieving the rank of Eagle Scout. My father died when I was 12 years old, so I went to work at an early age for New Jersey Zinc. They were good employers and good citizens, providing parks and baseball fields for the community

When World War II broke out, I was living near Allentown and working at Bethlehem Steel, making cannons for battleships. One of my fellow workers told me of his experiences at the Merchant Marine Academy. I decided to enroll, and

Ed Donner

received training for about five or six months on the TV Emory Rice. I remember in particular that sleeping in hammocks wasn't much fun.

When I was ready for active service, I was offered a choice of ships, one destined for Oran, in Africa, and the other for Murmansk, in Russia on the Arctic Ocean. That was a terrible time for Allied merchant ships in the Atlantic, so when I was assigned to a position below deck, I decided to resign.

A month later I was drafted into the army. I had artillery basic training at Fort Bliss. In May and June 1943 we were on maneuvers in Louisiana, in extremely hot weather.

It wasn't long before I was transferred to the 153rd Artillery Operations Brigade, which was ready to sail to Scotland on the *Queen Mary*. In November, 1943, when I was stationed near Cambridge, England, we could watch the American Flying Fortresses headed for Germany by day, followed by the British Lancasters at night. I was able to take a special course in radar in London.

At night, instead of hiding in bomb shelters, we would find a spot on an upper floor to watch the German planes flying overhead and our anti-aircraft guns responding. One night we saw our first V-2, which I mistook at first, for a German plane, hit by our own gunfire.

Two days after D-Day (June 6,1944) we were reassigned to a troop ship in Southampton, carrying 500-600 people. From there we transferred to landing craft, and landed on the Normandy beaches on June 15. We engaged the enemy around St. Lo, where I was an artillery forward observer. The Germans had mined the area, but unfortunately the first casualties I experienced were three GIs killed right in front of me by our own artillery fire.

The bridges were all destroyed, and we had no pontoon bridges, so we had to fjord creeks that were 30 or 40 feet wide. I slept in chicken coops, barns and foxholes. Though the temperature was in the 80's, the foxholes were cold. Sometimes I was lucky enough to find one I didn't have to dig for myself.

From Normandy we turned north to Brittany and Cherbourg, where the Germans had a submarine base. The Free French partisans, civilians in civilian clothes, were a great help to us. It took two to three months to march from there to Rheims. While in Normandy, we were attached to the first Army.

It took us two or three months to get from Cherbourg to Rheims. I was in Avranches when Paris was liberated. In Normandy, we had been part of the 1st Army, but were transferred later to General Patton's Third Army. En route we were within about 40 miles of the Bulge. I remember one encounter with General Patton, when we were required to pull off to one side to let his reconnaissance car pass. The plate with four stars was impressive. He was called "Old Blood and Guts," but we knew it was our blood and his guts. After the Battle of the Bulge ended, we were in Belgium for a month or two, and then moved on to Germany. Passing through Aachen and Koblenz, I was amazed by the damage our Air Force had inflicted.

When Paris was liberated, I was in Avranches, and when the fighting ended I was in Garmish-Partenkirchen near Hitler's vacation retreat. We then went on into Austria, but soon pulled back into Bavaria. I was then able to send my M-1 rifle home at no cost. I still have it.

While we were waiting to be redeployed, I was assigned to Lucky Strike, one of the camps named for cigarettes. Nearby was a camp holding 100,000-200,000 prisoners of war. They did all our donkey work for us, one of which was scrubbing the pots in the kitchen. I remember one incident when my buddy Frank Fratelli, who was Jewish, pushed a German officer into the latrine when he refused to use the same one used by enlisted men.

When it was my turn under the point system, I sailed home on the US Argentina. I was lucky to be bunked back a bit from the bow, which helped to make the trip smoother sailing.

Instead of looking for a job, I took advantage of the GI Bill of Rights to get a bachelor's degree in commerce and finance from Bucknell University. I went on to study for a master's at Lehigh University, but I never finished, because my GI Bill allotment ran out. During that time I worked part-time for Bethlehem Steel.

After graduation, I was married and moved to Newtown in 1953, where I went to work for US Steel, first as an expediter, and then was an operating practice engineer. Most of my career involved the operation of blast furnaces. I retired after 25 1/2 years, in 1979.

My wife is a graduate of Cornell University, and after twenty years of retirement, began work as a Pennsbury school nurse when our daughter was ready for college. That daughter now lives in California, where she works as a flight instructor. Our other daughter, a librarian, also lives in California, but she is no longer able to work because of severe chemical allergies caused by an overdose of formaldehyde in her work place. She cannot even fill the gas tank of her car or drive on the freeways where she is exposed to many exhaust fumes. Our third child, a son, lives in Colorado where he has a medical practice in spinal surgery.

We have seven grandchildren, one 30 years old, five in college and one in high school. They all enjoy my tales of WW II.

CHARLES FAGER

I was born on October 24, 1924, in Harrisburg, Pennsylvania. I graduated from William Penn High School in June 1943, was drafted on July 6, 1943, and was sent to Miami Beach, Florida for Army Air Force basic training, which was close order drilling, physical training, guard duty, and learning general orders. From basic training, I was sent to radio school at Sioux Falls, South Dakota. There I learned to receive Morse Code at 20 words per minute, and send at 12 words per minute. They also instructed the students in radio theory, and introduced us to airplane radios. Next was gunnery school at Yuma, Arizona, with 50-caliber machine guns. From there, I was sent to Plant Park, Florida, and assigned to a crew. Our crew

Charles Fager

shipped out to McDill Field, Florida, and started training on a B-17. After two months of training, we were sent to Savannah, Georgia, and were assigned to a B-17 to fly the northern route (Labrador, Iceland, England) to Italy. My excitement on joining a B-17 flying crew, and getting on the move, quickly became a sober understanding of the risk of flying missions. Our crew started flying missions in Italy two days after Christmas in 1944, the same time as the Battle of the Bulge.

I've been separated from my crew members and the Air Force for sixty years. Shorty Allison, who came from Texas, was our turret gunner. We broke Italian black bread and drank Italian red wine together on Shorty's 19th birthday, and I can't forget Munich, Vienna, Regensburg, Graz, Weiner, Neustat, Maribor, Mosebierbaum, and all the other targets, which were not cities, but battlegrounds five miles above those cities. There we became close friends. Somehow I lived and came home safely, but some of my brothers never made it, and will stay on foreign land forever.

The B-17s we flew on were *Pick Up*, *Our Baby*, *The Anthony J*, and other ships that only have numbers.

Our crew was assigned to fly B-17 *Pick Up* on Easter Sunday, April 1, 1945. We got up that morning, ate breakfast, went to briefing, put on our electrical heated flying suits, inspected the plane, and climbed aboard, waiting for take off. We had two options: either go to Linz, Austria, that had 200 flak guns, or Maribor, Yugoslavia, that had 35 88mm flak guns. We were in our plane waiting to see which place would be our target. We cheered when the flare went up for the smaller target. The bridge at Maribor was our target. We thought it was going to be a milk run. Our pilot, Lieutenant Dameworth, started the engines, and got into our position for take off. He popped off the brakes, poured on the horses. We started down the steel mat runway, and took off with our heavy load of three tons of 1,000 pound bombs. We joined our squadron and our bomb group, twenty-eight planes in all, seven from each squadron. We climbed to 10,000 feet, put on our oxygen masks, and continued climbing to 25,000 feet. After two hours of flying over the Adriatic Sea and part of Yugoslavia, we got on the IP and started to fly directly to our target, a bridge. We put on our flak suits and helmets. About five miles from the target, accurate flak started to explode throughout our bomb group. The Germans had flak guns on railroad cars and on top of mountains. We saw ships being hit by flak. At a briefing, Intelligence said there were few flak guns on this route. Harry McCurry, our regular co-pilot, didn't fly that day; he had gone to a rest camp somewhere. Our extra co-pilot had been a regular co-pilot on one of the ships that went down. When the extra co-pilot saw his regular crew hit and start to go down, he pushed the yoke forward to follow them down, but Dameworth stopped this action. The extra co-pilot was distraught. The bombardier said, "Bombs Away," and we rallied to the right. We were ship number 3. Out of a total of seven planes in our formation, 1 and 4 went down that day. Two ships floundered. Pilot Rackley of the 817th Squadron said, "the surprise of Maribor, Yugoslavia, where the sky looked like a replay of the lines from the Star Spangled Banner from heavy close enemy fire and many planes spiraling down ahead of us."

We got back to our field. Friends were killed in that mission, our nineteenth. Our plane had 179 flak holes. We came close to our last plane ride and mission.

Moore's crew was on one of the ships that went down in our squadron. While on a bomb run, flak knocked out the number 4 engine, and damaged engines 2 and 3 so that they developed only half of their normal power. The pilot and co-pilot were wounded. Dropping behind the formation, they headed for Zara, Yugoslavia. A fighter escort arrived to protect them. Pilot Moore was not able to get over the mountain to Zara, so they spotted an airfield, and his co-pilot turned in to land. While on the turn, number 3 engine lost more power, and he couldn't recover from the turn. The left wing struck a small hill, and the airplane crashed. The pilot and co-pilot got out, but the other crew members were killed and burned in the crash. The next morning, an English-speaking guerrilla met them, and they were evacuated on a C-47, returning to duty five days later.

I graduated from Gettysburg College in 1948 and the University of Pennsylvania Veterinary School in 1955. I started a small animal practice in Camp Hill, and in 1974 my brother Hummel joined me. In 1992 my brother and I sold our practice, but proceeded to continue working for the new owner for several years. Since that time my wife and I have enjoyed our retirement in traveling, and our grandchildren.

At one time I owned a small airplane, a Piper Arrow, flying it as far away as Alaska and Florida.

I was married on June 11, 1959, to Mary Kay Miller from Harrisburg. We have four children, two girls and two boys.

CHUCK FULTON

I was born in Minneapolis, and raised in St. Paul, Minnesota. I finished Central High School there at the age of 17. On my 18th birthday I was drafted. Because of severe nearsightedness in my left eye, I was classified as "limited service." I took basic training as a medic at Camp Barkley, Abilene, Texas. I was reclassified as "full service," but continued training as a medic. Completing my basic training, I then went to the University of Oklahoma under the Army Specialized Training Program (ASTP) where I took basic engineering courses. The schooling was rigorous with classes all day, five days a week, and exams on all subjects every Friday. We

Chuck and June Fulton

marched to and from classes, had daily roll calls, calisthenics, inspections, and bed checks, along with enforced study hours.

In February 1944, the Army shut down all such programs and assigned everyone to fill up Infantry Divisions being prepared to go overseas. I thus became a rifleman in the third platoon, K company, third Battalion 411th Infantry Regiment of the 103rd (Cactus) Infantry Division training at Camp Howze, Gainesville, Texas. There I trained as an infantry rifleman, earning a sharpshooter's medal, promotion to Private First Class (PFC) and became the third platoon's first scout and rifle grenade man.

In mid-September the Division moved to Camp Shanks, New York from where we departed for overseas in early October. Our troopship was a converted Italian luxury liner the Monte Cello. I was assigned all night kitchen police (KP) duty, which actually turned out to be a good deal. Reading the notes enclosed in egg cartons from the farm girls who had packaged the eggs was a highlight. They wished us well and some even included names and telephone numbers to call.

We landed at the famous French port of Marseilles, which had been captured during the invasion of Southern France in mid-August. It was still pretty much in shambles. After reorganizing and intensive training, the Division was moved by the same forty and eight box cars used in WW I to the foothills of the Voges Mountains. There we were committed to combat on November 11th, WW I Armistice day.

The first dead soldier I saw was a German medic. I used his body to hide from shrapnel as I underwent the first of many artillery shellings. I had trained in the summer heat and desert of Texas, but now I fought in mountainous terrain in bitter cold winter rains and snow. Our foods (K rations and C rations) as well as our clothing, initially, were inadequate for such conditions.

I mostly hiked, crawled, walked and ran up and down the mountainsides, almost always on the attack against retreating Germans. I rarely slept in a house or barn or any kind of warm shelter, being outside in a foxhole I had dug in the frozen ground.

Often times I was terrified by being shelled by mortars, artillery, and even screaming meenie rockets, as well as shot at by rifles, burp guns and machine guns. Our casualty rates were high. Of eight buddies from the third platoon that had gathered at Jack Dempsey's Restaurant in NYC just prior to shipping out, all were killed or wounded, including me. That I survived as long as I did---two months, was a miracle.

One time I vividly remember was when I literally walked through the *valley of the shadow of death*. We had been chasing the Germans all day. We then dug-in in the middle of a forest through which a road wandered, leading to a cluster of buildings some half-mile ahead. Patrol was ordered to investigate whether or not the Germans were posted in the village, or had retreated further on. The third platoon Corporal was to lead our BAR man, Harold Class, and me to survey the place looking for roadblocks and any signs of the Germans.

It took nearly an hour, moving slowly, cautiously, and as silently as possible through the edge of the woods along the road. The small clearing with its cluster of buildings looked wholly destitute, a dozen or so dark and silent small shapes. We slowly circled the place spying on it from just inside the edge of the surrounding forest. Everything seemed deserted with absolutely no signs of life. We were pretty much convinced the place was empty.

The Corporal said that he and Classy would stay on the entrance road as cover and backup, while I was to enter and examine some of the buildings close up. I inched my way in the dark. It too, was silent and deserted. So, then I went on to the next one. Nothing to see or hear there either. I thought I'd try one more before heading back.

OOOF! I bumped into something. Paralyzed, I didn't move. I stopped breathing. I broke out in a cold sweat. There was the black shape standing directly before me. I could just discern what looked like a German helmet. We both stood there—silent, motionless—frozen in time and space. Then, without a word, we each took a step back and turned away.

Slowly, then with increasing speed, I headed back down the road. As I dashed by my comrades I gasped, "There's a German patrol in there!" All three of us tore on down the road back towards camp as fast as we could go.

I will forever thank my lucky stars that that German soldier must have been just as surprised and scared as I was and that we both had chosen discretion as the better part of valor.

After we reported to the Sergeant, I sought out the supply clerk and told him I urgently needed a clean pair of underpants.

I got violently sick with gastroenteritis after gulping down a Thanksgiving meal, the first hot food in weeks. I spent a week in a field hospital, then returned to the company to find my best buddy Harold Class, had been killed the night before.

We crossed the border into Germany and attacked the Siegfried Line. In a communications trench leading to a massive concrete pillbox, both the third platoon's lieutenant and its sergeant were killed while next to me as we tried to attack.

When the Germans broke through in Belgium, initiating what was to be called the "Battle of the Bulge," the 103rd was pulled back and sent to defensively fill in the positions vacated by Patton's Army as it attacked to relieve Bastogne.

On January 11th, 1945, the 411th once again went on the attack and I and three buddies were all shot. Three of us by the same German MG42 machine-gun. I had thought that all except myself were killed. But later I found out that only Sergeant John Corey, whom I had tried to pull behind a tree when he was first hit, actually died on the spot. The other two had survived and discovering them to be alive was the highlight of my battlefield experiences.

I spent some six months in Army hospitals in France, England and the United States recovering and recuperating from my gunshot wound. The war in Europe ended while I was on a hospital ship returning to America. I was home on leave from the hospital when WW II ended. I was then assigned first as a clerk, processing returning GI's and then as a POW guard to return German prisoners back to Germany. With the help, initiated by my Dad, of the senior senator from Minnesota, I was finally honorably discharged from the Army on February 23, 1946. For my services I was awarded the Purple Heart, the Combat Infantryman's Badge and the Bronze Star.

My book, My Draftee Life, has more detailed information, descriptions, adventures and misadventures of my Army life as a draftee.

Out of the Army, I went to school under the GI Bill of Rights, graduating from the University of Maryland with a degree in Physics. I married June Kline of Allentown, Pennsylvania and we had two boys, Brian and Clarke. From them we now have four wonderful grandchildren. During the war June was in nursing school and had joined the Cadet Nursing Corps. As registered nurses had flocked to join the services, that program was established by Congress to provide nurses for the civilian hospitals and institutions and was under the Department of Public Health Services.

Professionally, I worked for 41 years for the US Government at the Naval Ordnance Laboratory, Frankford Arsenal. I tested rocket fuses for the Navy and managed the ballistic test range facilities for small arms weapons and ammunition for the Army. I served as Superintendent of the NATO North American Regional Test Center (NARTC) for the production acceptance of NATO qualified small arms ammunition.

My life has been, at times, demanding, terrifying, and downright dangerous, but it has also been exciting, adventurous and most interesting.

I am proud to have served my country in many ways and await that final Army ceremony--Taps.

BLAINE GARNER

Blaine Garner

I was born in Doylestown on June 15, 1912, one of six children. My father worked in a bank. After high school in Doylestown, I wasn't sure what I wanted, so I went for a year to Pierce Business School. A neighbor took an interest in me, and loaned me $6,000 for college expenses, which I was able to repay later. I took the pre-med course at Penn State, helping to pay my way by waiting on tables in term time and working for 40 cents an hour as a painter and road maintenance man in the summer. I went on to Jefferson Medical School, where I graduated in 1939. Members of our class were offered a commission in the Army reserve after two weeks at Carlisle Barracks. We all signed up. After a two-year internship in Abington Hospital, I was called to active duty in July 1941. I spent several months at Fort Meade in a unit that trained enlisted "medics" in first aid, handling patients on litters, and other routines for dealing with the wounded. In the fall of 1941 I worked in a tent hospital on maneuvers in North Carolina. I was on my way home to get married when Pearl Harbor was attacked. We were married on January 3, and in March I went to Carlisle Barracks for two months of indoctrination. In June, after celebrating my birthday, I learned that I had been reassigned to the Second General Hospital, a high-class outfit with Park Avenue doctors on its staff. At the end of the month we set sail for Liverpool. We set up our hospital in Oxford, where I spent two years taking care of the 8th Air Force. I was in charge of the admission, disposition and dispensary. A high point, in July 1942, was meeting the Queen of England at a nearby church.

I remember one soldier we admitted who should never have been drafted. He had an elbow immobilized at a right angle. He couldn't even hold a gun. I sent him home to the United States.

Just before D-Day, I was attached to the British "Desert Rats" as a medical officer. I remember trying to teach the British some sanitation, only to be dismissed as a Yank who didn't know much. The day before D-Day I saw the invasion fleet getting ready. We could also hear the bombers flying over to France to prepare the way for our invasion.

We arrived in France on July 23 and set up a tent hospital in Normandy, where we remained until December, when the hospital moved to Nancy. Before that I had been sent out on detached service, to a field hospital which was then serving American soldiers wounded in the Battle of the Bulge. My job was to give blood transfusions to soldiers awaiting surgery. They would have died without that blood. I looked after perhaps fifty a day. The surgeons were from St. Luke's Hospital in New York.

When I returned home at the end of the war, I had the option of using the GI Bill to finance further study in a medical specialty. But I thought I was too old to go on being a student, so I looked for a place to open a practice. My father thought I was stupid to choose Newtown over Doylestown. For a while, it looked like he was right. About the only doctoring I did was medical examinations for school children, for the three established doctors had all the business. As time went on, I got my share, not only of normal fees, but also of farm and garden produce that patients shared with me. I retired after fifty-five years as a general practitioner.

To keep busy these days, I do volunteer work at the Newtown Library. And my daughter-in-law recently introduced me to quilting. One of my quilts has been displayed at the Grange Fair. I also travel abroad with my daughter-in-law. We recently took a cruise on the Baltic, which involved quite a lot of walking when we visited ports. Two of my sons live here in Newtown, and one in York, Pennsylvania.

SAM GRAY

Sam Gray

I was born at 105 S. Chancellor Street, Newtown, Pennsylvania on February 25, 1910. I attended the Chancellor Street School, then George School for three years, and graduated from Mercersberg Academy in 1929.

Entering Yale, I joined the ROTC program and upon graduation in 1933 was commissioned a second lieutenant in the Field Artillery Reserve. In 1936, while a student at Temple University School of Law, I was commissioned in the 108th Field Artillery Regiment (155mm howitzers), 28th Division, Pennsylvania National Guard. In 1938 I started to practice law in the office of Arthur M. Eastburn, Esq. at Doylestown, Pennsylvania. In 1940 Martha Walker Dinsmore and I were married. We had four children, daughters born in 1942, 1944, and 1953, and a son born in 1950. The 28th Division was activated for Federal service on February 17, 1941. We were on our way to Indiantown Gap Military Reservation from the Carolina maneuvers on December 6, 1941. In February 1942 at Camp Livingston, Louisiana, the Division was triangularized (losing one infantry regiment and two artillery battalions), and I left it. While stationed at Ft. Bragg, I attended the Command and General Staff School at Fort Leavenworth, Kansas.

After attending the Field Artillery school at Fort Sill, Oklahoma, I was assigned to the 945th Field Artillery Battalion (155mm howitzers), school troops, formerly of the Georgia National Guard. The 945th completed preparation for overseas movement at Camp Gruber, Oklahoma. I sailed with the Advance Detail on the *Queen Elizabeth* to England in April, 1944. The Battalion followed in July. We drew equipment, calibrated the howitzers, boarded 2 LST's (landing ship tank) and 2 LCT's (landing craft tank), crossed the English Channel, landed on Utah Beach, August 12th, 1944. Assigned to the XII Corps of TUSA (General George Patton's Third United States Army), we participated in the dash across France and were in the Saarland when the Germans launched their Ardennes offensive (Battle of the Bulge). The march north to Luxembourg was characterized by fog, rain, sleet, and snow in that order. At times when we were west of the Army "Light Line," I drove with the headlights on for the first time in nine months. After the

Germans were driven north of the Sauer River, we remained in the vicinity of Consdorf, Luxembourg, for almost two months. Entering Germany February 26th, the battalion crossed the Rhine in March and finally stopped in Czechoslovakia on May 8th, VE Day. Although attached to XII Corps throughout, the Battalion at various times supported twelve different divisions, nine infantry and three armored. Between August 1944 and May 1945, members of the battalion had fired almost 60,000 96-pound projectiles (HE, WP & smoke), had 21 killed, acquired 78 Purple Hearts for wounds, and earned 104 Bronze Stars. Throughout the campaign a platoon from an AA Regiment provided anti-aircraft and anti-tank protection.

As Executive Officer (2nd in command), I spent most of my time at the CP (Command Post) and FDC (Fire Direction Center). I coordinated the anti-aircraft and anti-tank defenses, supervised paper work and assumed command functions in the absence of the CO. Having originally been trained as a "Horse Artilleryman," I found the speed and effectiveness of the motorized artillery in WW II most impressive. This was made possible by better and more efficient motor and radio equipment, together with the two "Piper Cubs" permanently attached to each battalion. On occasion the Corps might hit a target with 200 rounds at the same time in a continuous salvo.

On April 13, 1945 I was transferred from the Field Artillery to service in Military Government and took assignments from the legal section of G-5 TUSA, and later from the E detachment of Military Government located in Munich. Those assignments included: command of the Buchenwald Concentration Camp; screening inmates of jails to liberate those who might have been imprisoned for political views, inspecting military government units in Bavaria, and miscellaneous services for military government. From May 1 to June 11th I was in command of the Flossenberg Concentration Camp, located in eastern Bavaria, about four miles west of the Sudetenland, near Pilsen, Czechoslovakia. I had a tough decision there. The camp was quarantined for typhus. General DeGaulle sent his private plane to pick up a hero of the French underground who had been imprisoned there. I wanted to see him go home, as he was a wonderful person, but I didn't want to spread typhus.

Having been transferred to the 10th Armored Division in September, I landed at Hampton Roads in October, courtesy of the United States Coast Guard and the *SS Admiral Capps*, and was separated from the service with the rank of Lieutenant Colonel.

On January 1, 1946, Arthur Eastburn and I formed the partnership of Eastburn and Gray, which continues under that name with probably 20 lawyers, but I am no longer involved.

Since 1986 the survivors of the 945th have held annual reunions. I have probably attended one-third of them. The son-in-law of the S-3 has compiled and published a history of the battalion.

BILL HILL

Bill Hill

I was born on December 2, 1918 in Penn Lynn, Pennsylvania in Montgomery County. It was a little town between Norristown and Ambler, Pennsylvania. I came to Newtown when I was six years old. All of my schooling was at the Chancellor Street School in Newtown, from first through twelfth grade. I graduated from Newtown High School in 1936 and was president of my class when I graduated.

I married Frances Banks the day the Japanese bombed Pearl Harbor.

I was required to sign up for the draft and in February, 1942 I was drafted.

I left Newtown with a bunch of other fellows, including some from Langhorne. We got on the train at Langhorne station and headed for Fort Dix, New Jersey. We were there only a few days, when they started sending us to different places. I was not very happy with my first assignment in an engineering outfit. I really didn't know what to expect, and if I had to go to war, I wanted to be in some fighting outfit. As it turned out, I was assigned to the 383rd Engineering Battalion and was sent to Fort Belvoir, Virginia for training on how to build bridges. From there we were sent to Camp Polk, Louisiana, for further engineering training. Then we were sent back to Fort Dix, New Jersey, a staging area for shipment overseas. From Fort Dix we were sent to New York to board the *Queen Mary* for shipment to Europe. We landed in Scotland, and from there to Tewksbury, England for further training on how to build bridges.

I was still not happy with my assignment, but I was in the army, and had to do what I was told. Then one day there was an announcement posted on the bulletin board for anyone interested in becoming a military policeman. Boy, I jumped at the chance to become a military policeman (MP)! I was sent to a school in Scotland, where we trained with the Bobbies. I trained with them for about a year, and after passing tests was sent out on assignments. I ended up passing tests to be an MP, and they sent me all over England and Scotland. My first assignment was at the Eisenhower and Montgomery headquarters in London. Once we landed in Europe, I had a job of guarding 2,000 German prisoners in a stockade in Le Havre, France. On all four corners of the stockade there were .50 caliber machine guns, and all guards carried a .45 caliber pistol. When I took over, I had all machine guns removed. Here's how I felt. Some of the Germans didn't want to be there any more than I did. The rest of the American boys wanted to go home. They wanted the war over. They removed all the .50 caliber machine guns, and none of the guards walked into the stockade with a .45 pistol on. In a separate stockade, we had to guard 200 prisoners of our own troops who were deserters and AWOL's.

Some of the bitterest fighting occurred during the Battle of the Bulge. As an MP, I was directing traffic, sending oil tankers to the Air Force base. I happened to look down the road, and here comes a jeep carrying General Patton. I saluted him and he said, "Where are you going with those tankers, Sergeant?" I replied, "I am sending them to the 8th Air Force Base. He said, "I don't give a damn whose gas it is, I want it." Now who am I to argue with him? And I waved my hand for the oil tanker to go to his tanks. His tanks need gas. He got the gas because that's what I was told to do. General Patton was quite a guy!

I spent a lot of time tracking down soldiers that were AWOL and deserters in both England and Europe. One time I had to go to London to hunt down a guy. His name was Robinson, right in the vicinity of Piccadilly Circus, right in London. Two of us MPs walked down one side of the street, while two others walked the other side. Then two of us went down a stairway into a beer hall, a pub. There we found Robinson. Oh, he was having a good time. I walked up to him and said, "Robinson, how are you doing?" He said, "Oh my God, they would have to send you for me!" I said, "Okay, you gonna come?" He came peacefully.

The last big job I had was the Big Red one. In a parade, we escorted the guys that fought in North Africa through the streets of Paris, down the Champs-Elysees and through the Arc de Triomphe.

After the war, Booker Dingle got me a job at George School, where I worked for quite awhile, and then went to work for PEL-Mor Laboratories, in Newtown until I retired.

I have been a member of the St. Mark's AME Zion Church for 68 years, and have been a pastor's steward all during that time. I started the first black Boy Scout Troop in Bucks County. I have been a member of the American Legion of the Morell Smith Post #440 for a good many years, and its commander in 1986-1988. I served as the Memorial Day Parade Chairman for 13 years. I started the Veterans Day Observance in Newtown and helped with the annual Legion pancake breakfast for many years.

I am a member of the Trilumin Lodge of Masons #M89 of Langhorne.

Compiler's Note:

Bill died July 15, 2005 at 86 years of age, was given a military funeral by the Newtown American Legion, and buried in Newtown at the Lighthouse Hill Cemetery. He had two children: Rodney and Gerlyn Williford, eight grandchildren, and four great-grandchildren.

ERNIE KOSAN

I was born in Berlin, Germany in December 1922. My parents emigrated from Germany in 1926. They located in Dallas, Texas. I attended school there, and graduated from Reagan Sr. High School in 1941, in Houston, Texas. After graduating from high school, I worked in a steel mill in Houston, and after two deferrals was drafted in June of 1943.

I was given the opportunity to volunteer for the paratroops. I thought, "What the heck, you get extra jump pay", actually 50 dollars a month more, which was pretty doggone good in those days. So, I volunteered for the paratroops. I first went to a camp in Toccoa,

Ernie Kosan

North Georgia. They threw all kinds of crap at you, and if you took it, you're okay, if you didn't you're out. One of the first things that happened was that when I got there, it was early evening. I just got off the train. I landed in my bunk and they woke me up at three o'clock in the morning with everybody else and they sent us double timing up Mount Curranie. This was our first chance to prove ourselves. If you made it, you were ready for the next test; if not, you were out. The next test was jumping out of a tower, just with a harness on and you'd slide down a wire. And other things, like push-ups, running around the field, and things like that. They were just trying to separate the ones who were going to make it from the ones that didn't give a darn. After about a week, I was sent to a Camp Mackall in North Carolina, right adjacent to Fort Bragg.

The training for jump school was all preparatory, followed by 13 weeks of basic training. Then I went for two weeks jump training at Fort Benning, Georgia. Jump school training basically was three weeks. The first week was tough physical stuff. The second week was chute packing, and then jumping. The third week was basic training, which we had already done. There was a week of further training in learning how to land, learning how to collapse so you didn't break your legs. Then, learning how to collapse your chute in case the wind caught it and was dragging you on the ground. We learned basic things, just to survive. Each one of us packed his own chute, taking responsibility for his own life. We packed them for five qualifying jumps, and when you made those jumps, you got your wings.

For the first jump, we were very well trained psychologically. Most of us up to this point were ready. Those that might have been afraid were usually dropped from the program before this. My first jump was exhilarating, and by the time you made your fifth jump, and got your wings, you had it made.

We shipped overseas in late May of 1944 and landed in Naples, Italy. It was just before D-Day, Normandy, June 6, 1944. We were sent into battle in Italy for a couple of weeks, just to get our feet wet. Then on August 15, 1944 we had our first combat jump in southern France near the small village of Frejus, France.

What actually became our first real combat jump may best be described in this way. We didn't have to pack our own chutes, just the chutes with the equipment. I was a radio operator, and carried what was called an SCR-300, weighing 30 pounds. You had to pack all that stuff and get it ready to pack underneath the plane. We just sort of sat around the airport there, talking and wondering what in the world was going to happen. We'd already examined all the aerial photographs, and they even built models of the area where we were supposed to land. The Air Force hardly ever dropped you off in the area called the DZ, the drop zone, the assigned area that is close to where you were going to be fighting. We had been well-schooled about the drop-site. We finally boarded the plane. It was about a three-hour ride to the drop-site, at 4 o'clock in the morning. We anxiously waited for the red light to come on so that we could hook up our parachute rip chords. The door was always open. We waited, waited, and waited for the green light to come on. It was awfully foggy. Finally the green light came on, and out we went. It was really quiet. There was no banter back and forth. You couldn't see anybody else.

It was 4 o'clock in the morning. It was dead dark. No sooner did I land, than I heard someone walking toward me in the underbrush. I challenged him and he responded by saying, "I say there, have you seen anything of my chaps?" It was a British paratrooper. And I said, "No, I haven't. I just got here myself." He says, "well cheerio," and walks off. I collected my radio, and found the other fellows, including the lieutenant leading us. We were fortunate to be dropped on target and made our way to the bridge that we were supposed to hold for the landing forces from the sea, about six to eight miles inland.

We were in enemy territory, without meeting any Germans. We did our job. We got to the bridge. We watched to make sure there was no enemy activity coming over the bridge from inland, and just waiting for us to come in from the sea. Meanwhile, there was all kinds of naval activity going on, and that's pretty scary when you hear those great big shells overhead. It sounds like all hell is breaking loose.

We were in five major campaigns. Our outfit was called the "Battling Buzzards."

The war ended in May 1945, and I was detached from my old outfit, the 517th Regimental Combat Team, and reassigned to the 13th Airborne, but was given a choice of joining the 82nd Airborne because of my five campaigns. Berlin was divided into four zones occupied by French, Russian, British and the American troops. I chose the 82nd Airborne and we occupied the American Zone. Anyway, it was at that time I met a German Fraulein, and went on a few dates with her, even though we weren't supposed to fraternize with the German women. It was a big joke. You send a bunch of American GIs into a city with a bunch of young girls, what do you expect? Anyhow, as time went on I found myself falling in love with her, and she with me. So we got engaged. When I was discharged, and sent back home, she could not leave at that time. We couldn't get married in Germany because of the non-fraternization rule, so I had to go back home and wait for her. She came over as a war bride. I had to post a bond to make sure that in case it didn't work out, there was enough money to fly her back to Germany. But as it turned out, we did get married. We've been married now for fifty years plus, have five children and eight grandchildren.

Following the war, I was in the reserves, but was able to attend Rice Institute, now Rice University, under the GI Bill. I graduated as an engineer in 1950, and went to work for an architectural firm. Then the Korean War started and I was assigned a MOS number (Military Occupational Specialty). I worked as a speed radio operator, and code operator too. I was able to get a hardship discharge because of my family situation with a wife, two children, and a mother to support.

I worked for two years as a research engineer for the Minneapolis Honeywell Company. Then I worked for Rohm and Haas, in the engineering division most of my professional career, in Bristol and Philadelphia, Pennsylvania. I got a golden handshake and retired at the age of 63 in 1985.

I now live in Hammondsport, New York. It is located 20 miles north of the Pennsylvania State line in the Keuka Lake country.

Compiler's Note:
Ernie Kosan is mentioned in the book: Astor, Gerald "Battling Buzzards" The Odyssey of the 517th Parachute Regimental Combat Team 1943-1945.

History: The 517th Parachute Regimental Combat Team was one of the Army's first elite combat units. It was organized in March 15, 1943 and began its training in the backwoods of Georgia. It began as a part of the 17th Airborne Division and later joined forces with the13th Airborne Division. The 517th saw most of its combat in Italy, southern France and the Battle of the Bulge. During this short period of time they collected one Congressional Medal of Honor, six Distinguished Service Crosses, five Legion of Merits, 131 Silver Stars, 631 Bronze Stars, 2 Air Medals, 4 Soldier Medals, 17 French Croix De Guerre, and 1,576 Purple Hearts, at a cost of 247 killed.

The 517th was formally activated on March 15, 1943 and deactivated on February 25, 1946.

PAUL MACKEY

(as told by his daughter, Kirsten Fleisher)

My father was born in Ashtabula, Ohio on September 27, 1921, the youngest child of Finnish immigrants. He grew up in the same town, and graduated from Harbor High School in 1938, at the age of 17. After graduation from high school, he worked for several years at various jobs in New York City, Greensboro, North Carolina, and Washington, D.C. He attended Fenn College, now called Cleveland State College, in Cleveland, Ohio.

Paul Mackey

His high school days at Harbor High were happy ones. He received good grades without having to work too hard. He was offered a scholarship to Oberlin College Conservatory of Music, but turned it down.

At the time the Japanese bombed Pearl Harbor, he was listening to a car radio, so he knew it wouldn't be long before he entered the war.

In the summer of 1941, he returned home to Ashtabula for a vacation, because he knew it wouldn't be long before he would be drafted. Carmel, who later became his wife, had just graduated from high school. He tried to enlist in the Marines, but was turned down because of his eyes. He enlisted in the Army in September of 1942, and was notified to report for duty that October.

He left the Ashtabula train station and headed for Camp Perry, just east of Toledo, Ohio. After a long train ride, he reached Ft. Reilly, Kansas, and Camp Funston, which were both the home of the Ninth Armored Division, which he joined.

He was not given army clothes for several days. In the meantime, he was given many forms to fill out, and an aptitude test on which he scored very well, an IQ of 141, which influenced his future assignments.

He was given 12 weeks of basic training, which was mostly physical conditioning. They worked him hard from morning to nightfall. There was lots of calisthenics and jogging. Then he'd run 100 yards and walk 200 yards at a brisk pace, only to repeat the cycle. The 10- and 20-mile forced marches with full field pack on his back were the climax of it all. The guys that trained him were regular army and got him in great shape. The food was good. There was always daily inspection.

In the final weeks of his training, he trained with armored tanks and armored vehicles. It was obvious that the Ninth Armored Division was being prepared for combat.

At the end of basic training, he was transferred to Headquarters Company and promoted to T/5, the rank of corporal.

In the Spring of 1943, he took a test which qualified him for a full-time college education under the ASTP (Army Specialized Training Program). He also filled out another form to go to OCS, Officer Candidate School, and chose the latter. The board of officers talked him into going into the combat infantry, and he was sent to the Infantry School in Ft. Benning, Georgia. It was another long train ride from Ft. Reilly, Kansas to Ft. Benning, Georgia.

At Ft. Benning there was a special camp set up for those who had no infantry training. He was taken to Camp Wheeler in Macon, Georgia, about 60 miles away. The prep course was physically very demanding. He learned about various kinds of weapons, like water-cooled machine guns and 81-mm mortars. Men in his unit had to be able to take them apart and reassemble them blind-folded.

After a 90-day prep course and infantry training, he returned to Ft. Benning, ready for infantry school. There were many kinds of exercises including confronting problems in the field. On the 10th week of the 13-week training program, a recruiter for the OSS (Office of Strategic Services) was looking for recruits. He graduated as a 2nd lieutenant. With three others, he volunteered for the OSS, and after a short leave, was told to report to the Q Building in Washington, D.C., the headquarters of the OSS.

On his return from leave, his first task with the OSS was to become familiar with underground groups (guerillas). Much of the activity centered around the Congressional Country Club in Washington, D.C.. He underwent a rigorous physical training, including hand to hand fighting, with a knife. The karate and jiu jitsu training were violent. The major emphasis of his training was on how to use explosives effectively. His unit would be operating behind enemy lines. All he knew was that the OSS was an exciting and dangerous outfit, better than being a replacement officer for an infantry company.

In the spring of 1943, he left Charleston, South Carolina for Norfolk, Virginia and Camp Patrick Henry. From there he boarded a liberty ship, part of a huge convoy, for North Africa. Once he hit the Mediterranean, he had to keep alert for German aircraft. After almost a month at sea, he docked at Port Suez on the Canal. Then to Camp Huckstep near Cairo, Egypt, and then by train to Palestine. While there, he learned to use a parachute, training with the British near Haifa, Palestine. After five jumps, he earned his wings. Then his unit was shipped to Bari, Italy, and became Unit 2671 OSS Special Recon Battalion. He then got orders to go to Greece.

He flew from Haifa by aircraft to Tel Aviv to Italy, and Bari on the Adriatic Sea, and he stayed in a castle at Foggia, and then got orders to go to Greece.

Rather than parachuting into Epirus, he sailed across the Adriatic Sea in an LCI (Landing Craft Infantry), with supplies and explosives for the Greek Andartes, who were opposing the Germans in Epirus. His unit was finally going to war. In 1944, he stayed in the Romanov Monastery for five months while in Greece. His main assignment was to protect the bridge near the Fancari Plain. One of his unit's first encounters with the Germans was a raid on a small village occupied by them, where his unit destroyed a supply dump.

Paul and Carmel Mackey

During his six-week stay in the vicinity of Epirus, his unit ambushed a German patrol and destroyed a 100-truck convoy. They waited until they could trap the convoy in a narrow portion of the road, and with bazookas attacked them at both ends. For this service against the Germans, my father was awarded a Bronze Star.

These activities against the Germans raised a concern about some of our army's future activities. The Germans had posted a notice that for every German killed, they would kill ten Greeks, including women and children. They tried to be pretty careful after that, avoiding indiscriminate raids on the Germans because they took hostages and killed them as reprisals against the Cendartes.

He hoped to be home for Christmas, but when the Germans attacked our forces in the "Battle of the Bulge", it changed his unit's plans. He went to Naples, Italy to get a ship to France. Airborne replacements were needed, so he went to Naples on Christmas day in 1944. He was transferred to the 17th Airborne, and left by ship for Marseilles, France. From Marseilles, he was transported to Nancy, then to Metz in January and February 1945.

He was assigned as a platoon leader in an infantry rifle company, not knowing anyone and being thrown into combat conditions. This is one of the reasons he joined the OSS. He was assigned to the supply corps of the Division, and was selected to come on the staff, and relieved that he was not being assigned to a rifle platoon. Some of his group were assigned to a glider infantry or parachute infantry regiment.

Axis Sally warned the 17th Airborne Division that in their proposed landing near Wesel there would be a welcoming committee.

He was assigned to a glider that was towed by a B-24. When they arrived over the release zone, the men in the B-24 unhooked the cable too soon, and the glider immediately went into a nose dive. They weren't supposed to do that. The men in the glider were the ones that were supposed to unhook the cable first. The crew frantically worked to unhook the tow cable from the B-24, and when they did they were able to pull out of the dive before landing. Nevertheless, the landing was rough, with the nose shooting up in the air. Many of the men inside the glider were injured, and needed medical attention.

At that point the Germans were surrendering *en masse*, some 10,000, many of whom were young boys and old men. The war was over for them, but not necessarily for the American troops. There was still the war in the Pacific.

Many of our paratroopers were less fortunate, and were caught up in trees and shot to death. Casualties were especially heavy near Fluren.

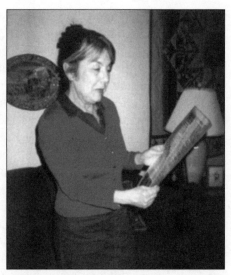

Paul Mackey's daughter, Kirsten Fleisher

All at once it was V-E Day and the war was over in Europe. Before heading home, he had some leave and spent some time in Paris enjoying V-E Day celebrations. Shortly after that, those who had enough points for discharge headed for Camp Lucky Strike to board passage back to the States from Le Havre. While there, he traded a P-38 for a German Luger. Within a few days, he boarded the *USS LeJeune* for the trip across the Atlantic to Norfolk, Virginia. From Camp Patrick Henry, he was sent to Indiantown Gap in Pennsylvania for discharge. He had been promoted to the rank of captain and signed up for the Army Reserves.

At that time he had 90 days leave coming to him, so he went by Greyhound bus from Harrisburg to his home in Ashtabula, Ohio. It was so nice to be home and greeted by his mother, and many other relatives and friends, and Carmel.

After his 90-day leave, it became necessary to find a job and further his education. In 1946, Hanna Coal Company in Cleveland, Ohio offered him a job, and offered to let him get a college education while working with them. He had already accumulated 40 credit hours while in the service, so he enrolled in Western Reserve University.

My mother and father were married in September of 1946, and moved to Cleveland to take up housekeeping.

My father had many jobs while working for Hanna. He worked occasionally with the deep mines, with coal preparation plants, and in the laboratory, gathered coal samples, and also prepared reports.

His next job, in 1955, was with Consol. He was made manager in the Syracuse office and lived in Fayetteville, New York.

In 1966 he left Consol and enrolled in a doctorate program at Syracuse University. While at Syracuse University, working on his doctorate, he ran into a snag, but got a masters' degree in communications, and took a job with Eastman Kodak in 1966 for a little more than a year.

In 1967 he was offered a position in the Department of Instruction with the Dale Carnegie Association, Inc., as an instructor of training conferences, and later became Vice President of Instruction. In 1969 he was appointed Manager of Research and Development. In 1984 he became vice president.

In 1986 he retired, but continued to work and write more on his own terms—outside corporate life.

He married Carmel in 1946 and they had four children: two girls, Kirsten and Paula, and two sons, Peter and Matthew.

Paul J. Mackey died on August 13, 2004.

WALT MAMMEL

I was born November 16, 1925 in Newtown, Pennsylvania. I graduated from George School in June 1943. I enlisted in the Army in 1943, and was put in the Army Reserve at 17, as part of an engineering program at the University of Florida. After three months, we were sent to Ft. Benning for basic training. The need for engineering diminished, and we were sent to the 86th Infantry Division in Louisiana. I qualified as an expert marksman with a .30 caliber light machine gun and was made first gunner.

Walt Mammal

The Division went to Camp San Luis Obispo, California for amphibious training to prepare for service in the Pacific, but in December 1944 the Germans launched the "Battle of the Bulge," which caught the Allies by surprise. The Division moved to Boston by train in February 1945, and sailed in convoy to Le-Havre, France on the "*USS Lejeune*". The ship had been a German tender, called the "Windhuk," for the pocket battleship "Graf Spee" in the South Atlantic. When the Graf Spee was destroyed, the Windhuk was scuttled but salvaged by the US. The trip to LeHavre was stormy, with some seasickness and occasionally the loud bang of depth charges. I was assigned to KP, washing pots and pans for 5,000 troops, and in retrospect I think the time passed much faster than it would have done if I had stayed in a bunk most of the day.

From LeHavre, I moved up to the Rhine River at Cologne in a truck convoy at night. The increasing noise and flash of artillery created rather vivid memories. After a week on the Rhine with the 15th Army, participating in some patrol activity, we crossed the river on a pontoon bridge and proceeded to split the Ruhr pocket with the 1st Army. The Germans were destroying the bridges to slow down the Allied advance. The infantry could scramble across the remains, but the tanks had to wait for the engineers. On April 12, 1945 we were pinned down in a field by German machine guns, until the tanks caught up with us. One tanker stuck his head out of the turret, and told us that President F.D.R. had died.

After the Ruhr pocket we joined Patton's 3rd Army driving into Bavaria. We frequently rode tanks 10 or 12 miles per day, and arrived in Ingolstadt on April 27, where Allied POWs, including fliers, were freed. We spearheaded the crossing of the Danube River in assault boats. We experienced no enemy fire on the river, but as soon as we hit the opposite shore German troops came out of fox holes and surrendered.

The war ended on May 8, 1945, and we had the opportunity, while in the 7th Army, to visit Hitler's destroyed retreat at Berchtesgaden.

The 86th Division had the unique distinction of serving in four of five American Armies on the Western Front. It was the first combat outfit sent back to the US, where we got a one-month furlough, and then proceeded to California. In Oklahoma, we heard of the atomic bombs dropped on Japan. The end sounded near. We sailed under the Golden Gate Bridge on August 28, 1945. We landed in the Philippines on September 20, 1945, which was after V-J Day. There we performed some guard duty. I was sent home and discharged at Fort Dix, New Jersey, on April 24, 1946. It was great to get home.

After more than two years in the Army, I attended Pennsylvania State University and received an electrical engineering degree under the GI Bill of Rights. My first job was with the Selas Corporation in the Philadelphia area. Following Selas Corporation, I was employed by the Western Electric plant in Baltimore, and later transferred to Western Electric Research Center in Princeton, residing in Yardley, and later in Newtown. While working for industry, Selas and Western Electric Company, I developed six patents.

In 1957, I married Rebecca W. Tiers from Germantown, Philadelphia, Pennsylvania. We have two sons, Albert Conrad Mammel and August Rath Mammel.

RICHARD MILLER

I was born on January 26, 1925 in Harrisburg, Pennsylvania. I have two younger sisters. My dad was a general medical practitioner and obstetrician in Harrisburg, Pennsylvania for many years. He served in WW I with a British medical detachment. After graduating from high school in June 1943, I tried to enlist in the Army Air Force, looking forward to a training program in electronics and radar. Passing all the other tests, I failed the one for color-blindness. The result was that I found myself boarding a troop train at New Cumberland Army Depot, Pennsylvania, on my way to Camp Fannin in Texas, between Dallas and Shreveport, Louisiana.

Richard Miller

This was summer, and it was hot! A very diverse bunch of recruits came from Los Angeles; Spokane; Brooklyn; Bronx; Wheeling, West Virginia; Harlan County, Kentucky; and only a few from Pennsylvania. Each of us received an education about the others' life styles!

The long hot summer under the boiling Texas sun, a record-breaker, was punctuated by many "character-building" incidents! If only one soldier in Company "B" screwed-up in any way, we all had to pay! The cursing top-sergeant from Kentucky would kick butt, humiliating us all. One favorite project mandated us (in evening "free" time) to dig an 8 ft. long, 8 ft. wide and 8 ft. deep hole, pitch in a cigarette butt, and fill the hole. Other punishments included "latrine" duty, and scrubbing the entire barracks floors (wooden) with toothbrushes. "They had better be spic-and-span, or it'll be your ass," the sergeant warned!

The mess hall was a totally new experience to all of us; varying degrees of satisfaction (or dissatisfaction) could be heard! Huge signs bearing: "Take all you want, but eat all you take." Hard for some recruits, but easy for me. We were often fed the famous, "SOS" (shit on a shingle, or creamed dried beef on toast).

Occasional local recreation centered around the "PX" with the 3.2 "Southern Select" Texas beer, and the huge jukebox going full-tilt with Bob Wills' "San Antonio Rose."

Along with classes on rifle nomenclature, use, and assembly, we had a rigorous regimen: up at 4:30 AM, with varied types of physical endurance tests.
"Forced marches" were scheduled at first with no loads, then working up to 20
miles with weapon and full field packs. Some carried carbines; mine was the 9
1/2 pound M-1 rifle. I well recall one extremely hot day (the low 100's) when a
third of our company literally passed out! Butts were kicked if one tried to fake it.
Prior to this, we were all given salt tablets. I threw mine up, but still had to keep
going! I was not one who could pass out!

Training was well along in the cycle before we were allowed evening or Sunday passes for town. My friend Ted and I chose to go into Tyler, a "dry" town,
while others preferred the "wet" towns of Kilgore and Gladwater. The Texans
everywhere showed friendliness and southern hospitality. Ted and I had been
invited to dinner at the Marvin Methodist Church in Tyler. Mrs. Whiteman, the
secretary there, had four or five of "her boys come every Sunday." I had never
before experienced real Southern cooking. We were encouraged to eat to the full
and play and swing to popular records of the day. Her home was our home! She
had welcomed so many of us who came through the training cycles, even took
time to write to us as we moved to other assignments, even overseas! Always,
there were encouraging notes to us, and the assurance of prayers.

When basic training was completed, some of us applied for the Government
A.S.T.P. program. I so desired radar and electronic training, but we were turned
down! The 526th Armored Infantry Battalion was frozen. Our so-called "Bastard
Battalion," being unattached, was chosen for a special assignment. This ended
my hopes for my chosen field. My friend at home had trained in the Navy for
radarman. The assignments for a top-secret program involved night tactics. Operating as armored infantry, our new project had us working with huge tanks which
carried specially equipped lights, flooding the terrain with effective "day light" in
order to blind the enemy. Our home for the next several months was a tent camp
in the extreme isolation of the Arizona desert. Wolves, snakes, gila monsters, not
to mention the long spines of the giant saguaro cactus were frequent enemies!
The latter can penetrate the GI boot!

Passes to town were few, and for four hours only! I was fortunate. A Jewish
boy in my squad invited two others and me to his home in El Sereno, California
in December of 1943. We were given blind dates for the famous Hollywood Pal-
ladium. We "wined and dined," and enjoyed the Big Bands!

Back at camp, our night maneuvers continued for several months. In December and January nighttime temperatures were near 30 degrees, and daytime (when
we slept) it would go to 75 degrees. Very dry desert conditions existed. The itch
of "prickly heat" was common. For recreation, I sat in on many pickin' and fid-
dlin' sessions as many of those boys from Kentucky and West Virginia were sing-
ing the "bluegrass" music. I really enjoyed it! Still do!

I'll never forget the night on training, when our half-track going at top speed threw a track! Just short of running into a giant cactus, our little fun-loving Greek driver came to a halt! He was grinning; no one was hurt, but it was a long time before he drove again!

Time passed. We had a Los Angeles APO, so we expected to ship to Japan or somewhere. However, suddenly the APO was changed to New York, and in March 1944, we were bound for Ray Ridge in Brooklyn. Nine days later we shipped out of Fort Hamilton on the "Sea-Train Texas" with all the tanks, half-tracks, and other gear on board. All of this equipment was under heavy wraps. As we sailed we were required to guard all of this high security gear in shifts. We knew not our new destination until we approached the Coast of Swansea, Wales, UK. Our new "home" became a rugged evergreen sheep pasture in fog-shrouded Northwest Wales. The largest city, Cardiff, was 40 miles away. Passes to closer antiquated villages were later given, where we heard mostly Welsh language in the local pubs. Our training continued with the tanks, but by June there were perhaps only three hours of total darkness. Fog and black mud permeated all aspects of our tent-camp.

Late in June 1944 (after D-Day) we shipped to Normandy, France without the tanks! A new assignment was in place. For the time, we "dug-in," using shelter-halves for our roof, staying in an old apple orchard for a few weeks doing "mop-up" work. The half-tracks which had been "stored" for a time eventually took us to Liege, Belgium to fairly decent quarters. The German-made V-2 rockets (buzz bombs as we called them) were frequent harassments in the sky, frightening all. However, their trajectories were uncertain, as they often missed their intended targets. We continued our "mop up." Then we moved into Comblain-la-Tour on the Meuse River. The old hotel there housed us, and we looked forward to a half-decent Christmas.

Suddenly, on a Sunday afternoon in mid-December, came an all-out alert! Ship out! The tragic counter-offense of the German Army had taken place! Three Ardennes Campaigns (known as "The Battle of the Bulge") were taking place. As the half-tracks were grinding away on poor roads, the weather had shifted from mild 40's to snowy-blizzard conditions as we traveled. A quick stop at one village provided some better cold-weather gear, but it was not enough - snow squalls, the blinding type, greeted us as we pulled into a small farm where the residents were checked out to assure us that these Belgian peasants were truly trustworthy, and not hiding Germans. This family was so happy to see us! They shared meager food supplies with us including bread, stew and some wine. The next day was clear and cold, a bitter deep snow having fallen. We proceeded to a point in the Ardennes forest, which would be our next "home." We "dug-in "using the well-known GI entrenching tool combination pick and shovel. Digging through the frozen ground, through hemlock roots, etc., was frightfully slow. And, in spite of our frantic activity, it was not possible to keep warm. Danger was present everywhere, the incoming missiles from the 88MM artillery pounding away, bitter wind, and the always-present danger of the enemy. Completing our dug-in positions, we lined our foxholes with any paper or greenery available. Hemlock and other conifers, which had been torn up, provided us with camouflage. Many crater-holes now white and blending with all the rest were easy pitfalls. Frostbite was common. By stuffing loosely tied boots with paper and other materials, I managed to escape the worst damage. From a high hill adjacent to our dug-in positions, we could see Malmedy in huge piles of smoke as it was being bombed by R.A.F. planes. On a day just before Christmas 1944, with bitter, still, clear cold, we were given orders by our Battalion Commander, Lt. Col. Irwin to "take" the small village of Stavelot on the hill and secure it. We had left our half-tracks behind many days before, so we were strictly on foot. Little known was the fact that Stavelot was full of Germans, both with Hitler jugend and the older ones - all fanatic and well-positioned. We were sitting ducks on the pristine white snow; we fell to our knees, and crawled, elbow and knees, on our "bellies" with our weapons. Suddenly, barrages exploded all around us. The snow turned to blood! Many close by were mortally wounded. Afraid? Surely! But I was fortunate to be able to survive this bloody battle.

Those who survived the carnage in hospitals later did not return to us. After a couple of weeks rest, the regrouped 526th was then included in Bradley's 12th Army Group. New assignments took us to Coblenz, Mainz and Cologne, the industrial section of Germany. In a laboratory at Wuppertol there were evidences of human experimentation. There were lampshades made of stretched human skin. Many other horrors were evident; even signs of biological uses in war were being explored.

Our mop-up and guard of this district took us to Cologne, a large city that had suffered close to 90% destruction from repeated bombings. There were many things I came to witness for the first time! Among the rubble were some individuals (not Americans) looting dead bodies. Heartening was the drive of some elderly women sifting through the rubble for whole bricks - then cleaning and hauling them away in a wheelbarrow! In the City of Coblenz was a huge wooden two story barracks-like structure, which had housed many workers for the industrial plants, like I. G. Farben. Most of these females were "displaced" persons from Poland, France, and Czechoslovakia, those who had not been sent to concentration camps. They not only supplied slave labor for the German economy, and war effort, but also were on demand for the "recreation" of German officers and troops. The city, having recently been captured by the Allied forces, had no more use for these deported ones. They were free (not controlled by us) and many, out of revenge and glee of liberation, went crazy, drinking and plundering on a wild spree! They did not fall under our surveillance, so to this day I don't know what happened to them.

From our duties in the Ruhr, we went to Wiesbaden, a beautiful city that suffered less destruction, except for the rail hub and related infrastructure, than most

German cities. We stayed there at the war's end until time for redeployment back home. It had been an important city S.H.A.E.F. for the Allies. We resided in what had been plush officers' billets having access to many amenities. I had a fine 3-band German radio and record player complete with stacks of German classical records. I had all of the J.S.Bach's "Brandenburg Concertos." Likewise I made use of a camera and a complete photo darkroom.

While still in Wiesbaden, I was saddened by another incident. There had been a number of replacements to our outfit after the battle campaign. One, a New Yorker, a German-born Jewish boy, had immigrated to England with an uncle before coming to the USA. Werner, who had sought combat with the Germans because of the persecution and loss of his family, was denied the revenge he wanted. Unknown to us was his utter depression. He vowed to kill himself (as many in wartime might have done), and with a Luger carried it out by blowing his brains! His good friend, Leo, another Jewish boy, with whom he confided, didn't even dream that Werner would carry it out!

We departed Wiesbaden, the "Rose Capital of Germany," for Namur, Belgium on the way to Camp "TopHat" for the long-awaited trip home. Those who had garnered the most "points" were sent home first. Purple Hearts, Battle Campaigns and other things were factored in, as well as time overseas. As I recall, I had 4 based on the Ardennes Campaign and time. We boarded an ancient World War I Liberty Ship, for a long, rough crossing. Most of the time I was too sick to eat, not from beer, but from the constant tossing! This is unusual for me (not to eat!). But I had company. It took better than two weeks at 11 knots. The sea was too treacherous around New York, so we were diverted to Boston and Camp Miles Standish, from which I traveled by train to Indiantown Gap for separation. Home after two and a half years was sweet. I was there for Christmas 1945.

A month after my separation from the Army, I enrolled in Gettysburg College, and after two years I tried to transfer to Penn State, but they were full. My application to the Capitol Radio Engineering Institute in Washington, D.C.. was accepted and I trained there for two years, 1948 and 1949, under the GI Bill. I spent six years in the Washington metro area as TV was being developed.

In 1953, I returned to Harrisburg and after a few small jobs, went to work for RCA Service Company. The area covered four counties within a 40-mile radius of Harrisburg. I spent about 25 years working with them.

My wife Nelda and I have been married 25 years, and we have five children, nine grandchildren, and two great-grandchildren.

We like to travel. One of our favorite spots is Acadia National Park, Bar Harbor, Maine. My wife and I have hobbies that keep us busy, and we like to garden.

We live outside of Boiling Springs, near Carlisle, Pennsylvania.

NORMAN O'GRADY

I was born on May 12, 1924 in a very small village in northern Vermont, where the Central Vermont Railroad had a junction with a line going into Burlington, Vermont, while the main line went north to Montreal, Canada. The village then took the name Essex Junction, the railroad being a major reason for the village growth at that location, within the town of Essex.

I graduated from Essex Junction High School in June 1941 in the smallest class ever, numbering

Sally and Norman O'Grady

15 students. We always said our class stressed quality rather than quantity. Of the 15 students, two were killed in WW II.

In the fall of 1942, I was a second year student, majoring in Electrical Engineering at the University of Vermont, in Burlington, Vermont. The Electrical Engineering students were contacted by Army recruiters with an offer of a special Army Signal Corps program which would enlist the student in the active reserve, and permit the student to stay in school on an accelerated schedule to get a degree, and then enter active service in the Signal Corps going directly into Signal Corps Officer Candidate School. This seemed like a good idea, so I enlisted.

I entered the service at Ft. Devens, Massachusetts in 1943 and was discharged from the same post in February of 1946.

Shortly after enlisting, the officers in the Advanced ROTC program approached several of us Electrical Engineering students and convinced us to transfer into the advanced ROTC course still remaining in college until we graduated. I did that, and this was an unfortunate decision, because five months later the entire ROTC program was disbanded and the Advanced course students became privates, and went as a unit straight into basic training. Those students who stayed with the Signal Corps Program stayed on through graduation. The next three months in the Summer of 1943 were spent in the Texas sun at Camp Wolters, near Ft. Worth, Texas.

After several weeks of basic training, a few of us decided to ask for a transfer to the Army Air Force applying for pilot training. These applications were rejected, as the Air Force at that time had more than enough flight cadets. We learned at the end of 13 weeks of basic training that we were destined to go back to college in the Army Specialized Training Program (ASTP). I was assigned to Lehigh University in Bethlehem, Pennsylvania, and placed in Advanced Term 5 of the electrical engineering program. I completed terms 5 and 6 before the program was suddenly terminated and the term 6 students in Electrical Engineering were sent to the Signal Corps school at Ft. Monmouth, New Jersey.

Upon arriving there each student was interviewed by a selection board for the officer candidate school. I learned of no person selected, and it was said that the school had a long waiting list. In any event I went through the Carrier Repeater training program, finishing in about three months. This program trained the student to operate and repair so-called carrier equipment designed to implement the modulation of telephone speech on radio wave transmissions and carry the voice several miles to another station where it was demodulated back down to normal voice for local telephone transmission. I was then assigned to a new Signal Service Battalion bound for overseas duty. After several weeks of waiting, our battalion shipped over to England in November of 1944. There, we again waited for shipment over to France, which came in March of 1945. The battalion was organized in teams of 24 carrier and radio specialists and each team was attached to an infantry or artillery unit to facilitate telephone communications between units of a division. From then on through VE Day we moved constantly through France, Luxembourg, across Germany and down into Czechoslovakia. Most of this time my team was serving with General Patton's Armored Division.

In June, since none of the soldiers had sufficient points to be returned to the States, our unit reassembled from all over Europe and went down to Marseilles, France to prepare for shipment to the Pacific Theatre. We boarded the transport Monterrey in July and went through the Panama Canal to the Philippines. While in the Pacific, near the Caroline Islands, Japan surrendered. The war was over.

My unit spent three months doing guard duty in Manila and then went up to Yokohama, Japan to await rotation home. In late January we returned to the States by ship as a unit and arrived in San Diego in early February of 1946. I was then flown to Ft. Devens, Massachusetts for discharge, and shortly thereafter was again enrolled at the University of Vermont under the GI Bill. I got to see a lot of the world, not under the best of circumstances, but fortunately saw no combat. It was an education to work with so many different people from all over the United States, and I grew up a lot, as a result. Not that I would want to do it all over again....

I met my future wife at a USO dance while in the ASTP at Lehigh University. Her name was Sara (Sally) McAllister. We dated off and on before I was sent overseas, and again when I returned to college after discharge. Sally went into the Cadet Nursing Program in 1944, and trained to become a registered Nurse at government expense. The agreement was, that upon the completion of her training, she would become an Army nurse, to serve during the war, wherever she was needed. She trained at Johns Hopkins Hospital in Baltimore, Maryland. The war ended before she completed her nursing program with the Government.

We did not get married until January 14, 1950, after I had been working for the General Electric Company for nine months and had a steady income. We have now been married 55 years and have three sons and three daughters, all with college degrees, and most with masters or doctorates. All are still married to their original spouse, and have given us 18 grandchildren. They are living in Colorado, Connecticut, Arkansas, Maryland, and two in Kentucky. My college degrees were a BS in Electrical Engineering and a BS in Commerce and Economics. I used up most of my GI Bill eligibility. I went with the General Electric Company right out of college and spent 35 years with them in various field engineering, field service, and product planning assignments. I have been retired since January 1, 1985, and have kept busy volunteering with several non-profit organizations and traveling to visit family.

CREED PALMER

I was born on June 1, 1918, and raised in mountain country, near Murphy, in the western part of North Carolina. We were about 90 miles from Asheville, and 90 miles from Atlanta. I walked three and a half miles to the nearest school, in To-motla. In warm weather, I walked barefoot. There were three grades in each classroom. My father died when I was in the 7th grade, so I quit school to work on our farm. I have a brother living in Tennessee, and three sisters, two in North Carolina and one in Indiana. I came from North Carolina to Newtown, Pennsylvania in 1940, worked for Ben Shaull for about six months, and then enlisted in the army at Fort Dix, New Jersey,

Creed Palmer

where I was housed in Tent City. We went for maneuvers to Tennessee, North Carolina, Arizona, and Missouri. On Pearl Harbor Day, we were bivouacked in the cemetery at Gettysburg. From there, we went back to Fort Dix. I received a 15-day furlough, during which my sweetheart and I went down to North Carolina and got married.

In December 1942 I left Camp Kilmer, in New Jersey, and crossed the Atlantic to Northern Ireland, landing in Belfast after 13 days at sea. The weather was terrible; all our lifeboats were swept overboard. Bunks had been installed in the hold of a cargo ship. Mine was the bottom bunk. We were a part of the largest convoy to cross the Atlantic, escorted by destroyers, and we didn't lose a ship. But we worried that the sea would destroy our ship, for it was awfully rough. On the crest of a wave, you could see the other ships of our convoy, but at the bottom, you thought you were alone. When we arrived at Belfast, 15 of our number had to be carried ashore on stretchers, because they had been knocked out by seasickness.

We landed on Omaha Beach on June 7, the second day, though we were not a combat unit. Our job was the repair of equipment, ranging from binoculars, transits, and small arms up to 155mm howitzers. We didn't exactly go by the book. We had learned from our own experience how best to do the job. We were held responsible for our own work. I could completely disassemble and then reassemble an M-1 rifle. People would ask me to explain my methods, but I just did it, and couldn't say how. When we got into Germany we came across some good steel rods that we could grind down into firing pins that wouldn't break. We carried with us a 75mm and a 105mm in good condition, that we would trade for one needing repair, and then fix the new arrival. What was usually needed was a new firing pin. We moved east, in close support of the infantry.

The 105mm howitzers had a range of about 15 miles. The 155s were bigger. There was also a 240mm howitzer, but they weren't much used. During the Battle of the Bulge, we got cut off for three days. We were given the task of rehabbing the rifles of all the guys that got killed in the Battle of the Bulge. We continued to move east, and were crossing the Rhine on pontoon bridges when the Germans surrendered.

Having enlisted in 1940, I had enough points to be one of the first to go home. I caught a troopship in Le Havre. We crossed the Atlantic in ten days. It was so crowded in the hold that we slept in shifts. So I decided it was better to sleep on the top deck.

I was discharged in 1945, and came home to Newtown, where my wife, who was born in Newtown, was waiting for me. We had met when I had worked on her parents' farm on Linton Hill Road.

After the war, I worked in a greenhouse for five years, then found a better job at General Motors. I lasted there only six months, when under union rules a man with greater seniority bumped me out of my job in Fairless Hills, where I rose from laborer to foreman for all the excavation, operating bulldozers and cranes. I worked for all three of the companies that were building that new town. (Levitown, Pennsylvania)

Next I was back in Newtown working with Plexiglas for Stan Sutton in the area underneath the old bowling alley. Then Bob Davis hired me for Newtown Hardware, where I worked for 30 years, and then retired.

WINSTON ROWELL

I was born in Dade City, Florida on November 21, 1922. I enlisted as a volunteer on January 2, 1942. I was assigned to the US Army Air Force and sent to England, where I remained from January 1943 to October 1945. I spent my entire military time overseas working in an Army PX. After my discharge in Sioux Falls, South Dakota, I returned home to Dade City.

My first post-war job was as a timekeeper in an orange processing plant for the Ocean Canning Company in Dade City, Florida. In 1949 I became a barber, and have pursued that trade right up to the present time.

A big change took place in Dade City to the orange growing industry due to the severe freezes of 1980, 1983, and 1985. This resulted in the orange growing industry moving 100 to 150 miles to the south.

My main contribution to the life of the Dade City area has been to help found and organize the Croom-a Coochee Baptist Church, about 11 miles north of town.

Fishing is my favorite pastime. Right now our streams and lakes are so low that the only fishing is in salt water. But it was in the Withlacoochie River that I caught my biggest fish. It was a 12 ½ pound large mouth bass.

I was married to Lois Sells on February 24, 1946. We have been together for 56 years, so far. Our two children, Tammy Louise and Randy, both live in Florida.

Compiler's Note:
Winston Rowell died in 2002.

ROBERT (KELLY) RUDOLPH
(as compiled by Bill Craighead)

I was born on February 8, 1924 in Carlisle, Pennsylvania. I graduated from Carlisle High School in 1942 and joined the US Army Air Force on October 12, 1942.

I attended Aircraft Mechanics School in Douglas, Arizona, and North American Aviation School for B-25 bombers in Englewood, California. I attended Flight Engineer School in Avon Park, Florida, and was a flight engineer on B-17s from Foggia, Italy, over Southern Europe. I was wounded in 1945, and received the Purple Heart. My missions included oil refineries, rail yards, airfields, and German troops in northern Italy. I also operated the top turret on B-17s with twin .50 caliber machine guns over North Apennine, Po Valley, Rhineland. Other awards include the Air Medal, Gunner Wings, Thompson submachine gun expert, Central Europe Victory Ribbon, WW II American Theater Ribbon, and the EAME Ribbon with four Battle Stars. I flew a total of 34 missions. I was discharged December 12, 1945. I worked at Olmsted Air Base and the New Cumberland Army Depot Helicopter Unit as a quality control inspector and aircraft crash investigator.

I married Doris Snader in 1947. We have two children, a son Jeff and a daughter Sandra, five grandchildren, and nine great grandchildren. I am a member of the Mt. Holly Evangelical Lutheran Church, and a member of Cumberland Star 197, F&AM. I was a 32nd degree Mason of the Harrisburg Consistory and belonged to the Harrisburg Zemvo Shrine. I was a life member of the Mt. Holly VFW.

Kelly Rudolph

Doris Rudolph, wife of Kelly.

Compiler's Note:
Robert (Kelly) Rudolph died in 2005.

HARVEY AND HERBERT SMITH

(as written by Herbert Smith)

My twin brother, Harvey and I were born in Mt. Alto, Pennsylvania on June 19, 1924. We lived there for three years, and then were adopted by Jean and Charles Smith, with whom we moved to Gettysburg, Pennsylvania. We attended Gettysburg Public Schools, and graduated in June of 1942. My college life at Gettysburg College was interrupted when I enlisted in the Army Reserves, and subsequently was called to active duty in February 1943. After finishing basic training at Camp Wheeler, Georgia (our Training Battalion number 12 was the first to be made up mostly of teenagers), we were sent to North Georgia Junior College for training as engineers in the Army Specialized Training Program. This lasted through the summer, when the program was discontinued. We returned to Camp Wheeler where, after a couple of weeks, we were sent to Camp Rucker as fillers for a new field artillery unit being formed. We remained with the 284th Field Artillery Battalion until I was wounded April 10, 1945. Harvey and I had been together all through the war. After I was wounded, he remained with the same outfit until the end of the war.

Herbert and Harvey Smith

I find it difficult to remember many specifics about my war experiences. Our outfit was assigned to the 3rd Army 20th Corps, just in time to help liberate Verdun. We are listed in their gold book as heroes of Verdun. We helped liberate Paris (not allowed in though), followed by a trip across France with General Patton. What a blast! This trip almost didn't happen. Because of a missed communication, we continued on through several small towns, where we were greeted as heroes, only to find out that we were behind enemy lines. After an uneasy night, we finally got back to our lines.

As a voice radio operator in Headquarters Battery, much of my time was spent working in the FDC (Fire Direction Center), getting information from forward observers for the personnel of FDC to use to set up fire missions for the gun batteries. When not in FDC, there was always maintenance of equipment. Being part of a liaison crew that worked closely with the infantry and cavalry, to whom we were assigned, we set up relay stations (three of us in a jeep out in front of the outfit, but behind the infantry), to find a spot where we could hear the forward observer, and relay his data to the FDC. I remember one time, as we were getting set up, when the German artillery spotted us and started firing. We were able to get inside a well-built power station building, so no harm was done. They wasted 10 to 12 rounds, but only managed to take off a corner of the building.

I have always found it difficult to compare my experiences during the war with those of others. I was lucky enough to have my MOS numbers changed from rifleman to radio operator (voice), and be assigned to a headquarters battery in

Harvey Smith

the field artillery. That alone was enough to change my entire war experience. While we in the artillery were subject to counter-battery fire, aerial bombing, and occasional small arms fire, it was not on a daily basis. Our living conditions were luxurious compared to many. Being a Headquarters Battery wc, by the very nature of our work, needed light and shelter. Consequently, we were often housed in barns or cellars, not the Ritz, but better than fox holes!

Most of my memories come back as unrelated incidents. For example, there was a day when several of us were tired of being dirty, and decided to go for a swim in the Moselle. That ended in a hurry, for shells started to come across from the Germans. We thought they were after us, even though none hit anywhere near us. We never did finish our bath.

Another highlight was the visit of the doughnut girls. Unless you were there, you have no idea how great it was to see and talk to "a gal from home." Those "girls" were willing to risk being wounded or worse, to bring a break in the war to a bunch of dirty, smelly GI's, and to take time to sit, talk and listen to us. I don't know if it is true or not, but I was told that one gave me a blood transfusion in the field hospital after I was wounded. I like to think it was true.

I remember one time when Headquarters Battery was positioned in a small French town, where the two faces of the war were clearly shown to us. Here we were, giving the gun batteries the coordinates for a fire mission, while from outside of the tent we could hear the voice and laughter of the town's children playing. Moments like that make one wonder what the war is all about.

It was in the same village that I got into trouble. While on guard duty one night, a door across the street was opened, and light poured out as a man stepped out. I yelled at him to close the blankety-blank door, and he did it. The next morning, I had to report to the Battalion Commander. He said that what I did was right, but the next time to be more careful how I spoke to him. You can be sure I was most respectful after that!

I remember another day that brought the war home to me in a very graphic way. Being in the field artillery, we were not accustomed to seeing the result of our actions. One day, however, when we were changing positions, we passed an area we had shelled the day before. On the run across France into Germany, we had seen dead German soldiers, as well as a few GI's. This didn't prepare us for what we saw here. The Germans were getting ready to eat when the shells hit. Some were in their fox holes, while others were beside theirs with their mess kits, all dead. What really impressed us was the fact that they were just like we were, different uniforms, but young men doing what they were trained to do, and who were in the wrong place at the wrong time.

Finally the day I'll never forget ....April 10, 1945. I was part of a liaison party attached to the 3rd Cavalry Group. We were on the road changing positions, when German airplanes spotted us. Where they came from this late in the day, we will never know. As luck would have it, they hit the convoy right where we were. If I think about it, I can still hear the noise of the planes, the machine guns, and explosions as they dropped fragmentation bombs right in the field where we

were. The next thing I remember was being worked on by the medics, and then being loaded into an ambulance, just before the morphine took effect. I remember complaining about the dirt falling in my face from the litter above me. This incident started me on a 13 months' stay in Army hospitals, before being discharged, with a new leg and a great respect for the Army doctors and nurses who treated me.

One of my best memories to come out of the war is knowing the men of the 284th Field Artillery Battalion. We were strangers

Herbert Smith

when the outfit was organized in 1943, but by the time hostilities had ended in Europe, these "strangers" were good friends and comrades. We could count on them to be there when we needed them. We formed a camaraderie that has lasted over the ensuing 50-plus years. That it is as strong as ever today is evidenced by our monthly newsletter and well- attended yearly reunions. Sadly, though, the number able to attend gets smaller every year. The official radio code name of the battalion was "Helpmate," the pride of the 284th. From that expression came our motto, "Helpmate Ready." That meant that we were always ready for any task asked of us. To this day the men of the 284th still consider themselves "Helpmate Ready."

After discharge from the Army, I returned to college, under the GI Bill and earned a degree in Psychology/Education from Gettysburg College in 1949. While in college, I met Betty Minnich, and we were married after graduation. After earning a Masters Degree in Psychology from Temple University in 1951, we moved to West Chester, Pennsylvania, when I took a job with the Pennsylvania Office of Vocational Rehabilitation, working with the handicapped. I stayed with them as a counselor and supervisor until retiring in 1984. We then traveled this country and Canada off and on for eight years in a motor home, and finally moved to a life-care community, where we have been for ten years. We have four sons, and five grandchildren.

My brother, Harvey Smith, after graduation from Gettysburg College, worked for the State of Pennsylvania in Harrisburg. He started with the Civil Service and then transferred to the Welfare Department where he worked for almost 40 years until his retirement. His wife's name is Anne. They have two children, a boy and a girl. Until recently, they lived in Mechanicsburg, Pennsylvania but now live near one of their children in McMinnville, Oregon.

Compiler's Note:

In 1938, in Gettysburg, Pennsylvania, Harvey and Herbert Smith, as Boy Scouts, at the age of 14, assisted the Civil War Veterans in celebrating their 75th anniversary of the Battle of Gettysburg.

KINGDON SWAYNE

I was born on November 26, 1920, in my parents' apartment in Drayton, the older boy's dormitory at George School. I graduated from George School in 1937 and Harvard College in 1941, then worked for a year at the General Electric Company in Schenectady New York. As a Quaker, it would have been easy for me to be a conscientious objector. But I believed Hitlerism was a greater evil than war, so I was drafted and sent to Camp Croft, South Carolina for basic training. There I was recognized as potential officer material, and joined a group of VOCs (volunteer officer candidates), most of whom were married college graduates who chose not to wait to be drafted, but to enter a fast-

Kingdon Swayne

track program that would send them to infantry Office Candidate School (OCS) right after basic training. We stayed together as a group through OCS and our subsequent assignment to the 328th Infantry Regiment of the 26th Infantry Division.

The 26th was the Massachusetts National Guard division. One of its regiments had been assigned to guard the Atlantic coast. That regiment remained on duty there, meaning that the division needed a new regiment to be complete. The number chosen for us had been, in World War I, the regiment of Sergeant Alvin York, the most decorated veteran of that war. The 328th was reborn to honor him.

In August 1944 we sailed for England. In September we landed in France, entering that country, without opposition, over the Normandy beachhead used on D-day, June 6. We became a part of General George Patton's Third Army, which took a wide swing to the south and east that surrounded much of the German force in northwestern France and forced its surrender. Our first encounter with Germans was in Metz, where some German forces had occupied several medieval castles. We starved them out fairly quickly, while at the same time filling up our ranks with raw recruits from the States, one of whom was Stuart Whittam, from Newtown.

We were essentially in a reserve status. That made us the prime candidates to respond to the "Bulge," a last-ditch German effort, in Luxembourg, to interfere with the Allies' progress eastward. The Grand Duchess of Luxembourg, incidentally, was at that time living in Middletown Township in what is now Core Creek Park. Her home was a stone farmhouse on a site at the bottom of what is now called, in her honor, Lake Luxembourg. The Allied strategy in Luxembourg was very successful, and the Germans soon retreated east of the Rhine.

While waiting for temporary bridges to be built across the Rhine (the Germans had destroyed the old ones), we holed up for several weeks in the industrial city of Saarlautern. It was there that I acquired the wounds that earned me a Purple Heart. I was inside a building when a piece of shrapnel came through the window. It struck my right leg near the knee, and a piece of window glass struck my left leg, also near the knee. The wound in the right leg was larger, but the one in the left leg was dirtier, so it became the chief problem. The problem would have been much worse a few years earlier, but in about three weeks penicillin made me whole.

Strangely, I was really anxious to get back to the front. Fortunately, by the time I did so, German opposition had all but collapsed. The mission was now to travel east as rapidly as possible, so that the Western Allies would end up with more of Germany and Austria (we were in the latter) than would the Russians.

I managed the trick of arriving home in Newtown at 11:55 PM December 31, 1945. I had, while in Europe after the war, taken and passed the written examination for the Foreign Service. An oral examination in Washington was successfully passed in June, and I went home to await the call to service. To keep boredom at bay, I took a job with the operator of a garage and filling station in Newtown. I was inexperienced as an auto mechanic. My main *faux pas* was the over inflation of the tires of the first car I serviced. But I was able to be helpful to my boss by setting up for him a good set of accounts, which I then maintained.

In June I went to Washington for several months of orientation, ending with an assignment to London (1946-48). I started there in the consular section, where our main job was to issue immigration visas to the thousands of GI brides waiting to join their husbands. I take some pride in having come up with a bright idea to bring order to a chaotic mess in our mailroom that had been precipitated by someone's decision to schedule appointments for the brides not more than two weeks in advance. Those without appointments kept writing to us, begging us to schedule them. I cut the Gordian knot by giving every waiting bride an appointment, even though that meant going six months into the future. The flow of begging letters ceased, and we could get down to our proper business of speeding the brides to their husbands.

Later in the London assignment I worked in the Ambassador's office. One of my tasks was to maintain his file on the Berlin airlift, a major US-UK joint operation at the time, supplying Allied forces in West Berlin when the Russians cut off access to them by land. The US commander in Berlin needed to know the decisions made in London, so one of my tasks was to relay them to him, in code, via US military radio. To get priority on the line, I had to identify myself as the Ambassador.

Kingdon Swayne and Virginia Lloyd

Toward the end of that tour there was a gathering of Allied leaders in Paris to plot our on-going strategy against the Russians. The Paris embassy's records were inadequate, so I was called to come from London with *our* set of records. A special airplane was provided to carry them and me.

After that giddy experience with high policy, my next assignment was to deal with the lowest of the low—applications for recognition as American citizens by Chinese who claimed to be the sons of fathers who had migrated to America and become citizens. The wives of the migrants remained in China, and every two years or so the husband would return to beget offspring. The offspring were quite remarkable: 90% were male, and, in a land where infant mortality was perhaps 50%, none of them ever died. It was a scam of massive proportions. The details of how we broke it would be tedious, but break it we did.

On my way home from that China assignment (1949-51), I spent several days in Japan. I was fascinated by many aspects of the country. After a year at my next assignment, at a boring job in the boring city of Toronto, Canada, I decided to break out of the rut by signing up for Japanese language and area training. This began, of all places, at Yale (tough on a Harvard graduate!). It led to what became the heart of my experience as a diplomat, Japan-related service in Japan or in the United States from 1953 to 1963.

There were three major high points in that decade:

1) My assignment as Principal Officer of the American Consulate in Sapporo, which was a key to my brief listing in *Who's Who in America*. Their criterion for including Foreign Service Officers was those in Class 3 (the highest I achieved) who had served as Principal Officers.

2) My service on a Kennedy White House Task Force to address issues arising over Okinawa. Among other things, I was the sole author of a press release,

carried *verbatim* on the front page of the New *York Times,* outlining future American policy for that strategic bit of real estate.

3) Service in the Kennedy White House as a Japanese-English interpreter, at a luncheon honoring the Japanese Prime Minister. I was assigned the task of translating conversation between the Prime Minister and the two ladies he sat between—Jackie Kennedy and Mamie Eisenhower.

My reward for service at a high level was an assignment to the Air Force War College, a step toward top-level service in the State Department. That led to my final assignment as head of the political and economic sections of our embassy in Rangoon, Burma. The high point of that service was the week when the Ambassador and the number two man were both out of town. That put me in the exalted position of *charge' d'affaires* for a brief period.

At the end of that service, I retired with a "golden parachute," a pension that was not only indexed for inflation but free of federal income tax. My intention was to come home to Newtown and seek a job teaching at the newly established Bucks County Community College. The "exit counselor" at the State Department told me about a program at Lehigh University that was designed to retread early retirees into community college professors. After Harvard and Yale, Lehigh might sound like the boondocks, but the fact that my brother Kenneth was a graduate made it wholly acceptable. My time there was well-spent.

I served at the community college from 1967 to 1987 as a professor of history and political science, retiring by my own decision when I concluded that at the age of 66 I could no longer do the job to my own satisfaction.

A new job was waiting, in the role of archivist and historian at George School, which was looking ahead to its centennial celebration in 1993. The school was quite willing to take a chance that a man who had never written a book would do a good job on its centennial history. I cannot be shy or modest about the result. It is generally thought of as the best of its kind. I place it #1 among my contributions to the world of books, in fact, as #1 among my achievements. Incidentally, its success led me to undertake histories of two other Quaker institutions in Newtown. I have done a centennial history (1897-1997) of the Friends Home in Newtown, where I now live. I also wrote the 50-year history (1948-1998) of Newtown Friends School, whose founding principal was my mother.

My service at George School continues to the present. I have a dollar-a-year contract, an office equipped with a computer (on which this is written), and decorated with photographs, artwork, and the occasional odd bit of memorabilia. My favorite picture dates back to my own era as a student. It is a tinted photograph of a performance, by marionettes, of A *Midsummer Night's Dream,* the creation of a hobby group, one of whose faculty advisers was James Michener, the well-known author, a teacher at George School from 1933 to 1936.

I was officially retired from George School in June of 2006 after 15 years of service.

JOE TURNER

I was born in 1926, in Flourtown, Pennsylvania into a family with eight children, four boys and four girls. We were very poor, and moved frequently. I particularly remember one house in Mozart, a large stone house on a 20-acre farm, with no plumbing, and a well that often ran dry. If we had had the money, we could have bought it for $2,500, but we could just barely raise $10 a month for rent. It was better after my brother Jack got a job in a hosiery mill at $18 a week. I remember selling a salve from door to door, on my bicycle. I spent the $3.50 I earned for a .22 rifle from Sears.

I wanted to follow my two brothers into the Navy, so in August 1944, I volunteered at age 18, hoping to get my choice of services. But I ended up in the Army, which

Joe Turner

might have been a blessing; I could have been killed in the Navy. After 17 weeks of basic training at Camp Wheeler, in Macon, Georgia, I tried to join the paratroopers, but was assigned instead as an infantry replacement with the 94th Division for a man lost in the Battle of the Bulge. Moving toward the city of Trier, I was wounded shortly after we crossed the Rhine. Later I was awarded the Purple Heart. Because the wound was minor, I was hospitalized in France. When I returned from the hospital, after two or three weeks, the war was still going on, but my unit had been assigned to occupation duty in Germany.

The Rhine crossing was terrible. The engineers kept trying to put a bridge across, but the Germans destroyed it every time. General Patton finally decided to use boats for the crossing.

Another hazard we faced was the shoe mine. It holds a quarter-pound of TNT and looks like a shoe box. If you step on one, it blows your foot off.

I took German corpses in stride. It wouldn't have bothered me a bit to sit on a pile of German corpses and eat my lunch. At the same time, I felt badly when I heard that some German soldiers who had surrendered to us were taken off and killed.

At the end of the war, the 94th Division was deactivated, and I was reassigned, first to the First Division, and later to the 70th Tank Battalion. I became the gunner on a medium tank, and was promoted to corporal. We were assigned to Czechoslovakia. There I met a Russian for the first time. We had replaced them as occupiers. They hadn't moved very far, so they used to come back in the evening to visit their girl friends. One of them wanted an American uniform, so I agreed to trade a uniform for his 25-caliber automatic pistol.

When we returned to Germany, I learned that we were allowed only one souvenir weapon. I had two, and wanted to keep them, so I removed two packs of cigarettes from a carton, replaced them with a pistol. But when I returned from a trip to Switzerland I discovered that it was missing. The Supply Sergeant said he assumed my roommate had taken it, but he couldn't prosecute the roommate without also prosecuting me for illegal possession of a weapon. So I brought only one of them home.

One fellow soldier was showing me a 25-caliber pistol, didn't realize it was loaded, and accidentally shot me in the belly. After a stay at the hospital, I returned to my unit, now in Czechoslovakia. I finally got a 25-caliber automatic.

Before I went to Czechoslovakia, I was assigned to guard high level prisoners. Hermann Goering was one of them. We were concerned that he would commit suicide, so whenever he covered his head, we rushed in and uncovered it, to be sure he wasn't about to kill himself. He told me that he believed he was merely a loyal German fighting for his country, not a war criminal like Hitler. He refused to give autographs as long as he was a war criminal.

I had brought home with me a dollar bill, signed by Goering, that I had kept hidden during my service in Europe. When I returned home, I gave it to my mother to keep as a souvenir, but she mistakenly put it with her other money and spent it.

BEN TURPIN

I was born at home in Trenton, New Jersey, on July 18, 1918 with a twin brother, who passed away at the age of 57. He was a machinist with Delaval when the war broke out, and he was drafted. His job was repairing tanks and other vehicles that needed attention after participating in landings such as the one at Guadalcanal. We moved to Morrisville when I was in third grade, into a large house occupied by three aunts who went out to work at the rubber mill while my mother kept house. I graduated from high school in 1938. My first job was at C.V. Hill, who made commercial refrigerators on Pennington Avenue in Trenton.

The year before, I had joined my friends (Frank May and "Speed" Kent, who shared my interest in horses) in enlisting in the regimental headquarters battery of a horse-drawn 112th Field Artillery Regiment in the New Jersey National Guard. We were required to drill once a month, but were per-

Ben Turpin

mitted to go over every weekend and ride the horses. After a three-year hitch, I re-enlisted, was assigned to Fort Bragg, North Carolina. Then I went briefly to Officers Candidate School at Fort Sill, Oklahoma. When I was asked whether I wanted to be there, I said, "No." So they sent me back to my regiment, where I remained throughout the war.

Shortly after Pearl Harbor, we became motorized, and also became the headquarters battery of the 112th Field Artillery Regiment. Our unit moved to Camp Polk, Louisiana, then to Fort Jackson, South Carolina, and toward the end of the year to New York, where the *Queen Mary* carried us to Europe.

There were three or four battalions in our regiment. The regulars were a 240mm howitzer battery, code-named "Helpless," an 8-inch howitzer battery, code-named "Loved Not," and an 8-inch battery, named "Wyoming." The fourth one, with us off and on, was the 18th Field Artillery Battalion, which fired rockets. The rockets were very effective in laying down a lot of fire, maybe twice as effective as the regular battalions. But they also produced a trail that made it easy for the Germans to target them in return.

We crossed the English Channel into Normandy several months after D-Day.

I had a fascinating encounter in Normandy with a German soldier. He was about 40 years old, and our prisoner. He knew his way around trucks, and cheerfully helped us repair ours. But they kept breaking down. Our response was to take the turrets off tanks and use them to tow our howitzers. This worked, because we could get parts for the tanks.

Our big guns were 240mm, and very accurate, with a 4-8 mile range. In the time between the firing and the explosion you could drink half a cup of coffee. We learned that some of our targets, small bridges in the Alps, had been built by the Romans.

Our guns killed a lot more Germans than the infantry could kill.

We originally laid telephone wires in ditches beside the roads connecting our forward observers to our guns. But we learned that our de-mining crews would throw the mines they found in the roads into the ditches. Several of our wire-layers lost legs as a result.

Together with the First French Army and our 3rd Infantry Division, we chased the last German unit out of France and across the Rhine. It was a bloody battle, especially for our infantry. There was a railroad tunnel just across the Rhine from our position, where the Germans had a large artillery piece that they would pull out, fire at Colmar, and then return it to the tunnel. We were working with a French Observation Battalion, whose members identified the location of German guns by measuring the time between the flash of light and the sound. We could then return the fire accurately.

We also had the pleasure of working with a combat team of Japanese-Americans, who won more ribbons and medals than any other outfit.

We also encountered some German soldiers who had been taken prisoner when their unit was outflanked by Patton's army. Many of them ended up in the United States, and after being repatriated at the end of the war turned around and came back here to live.

The driver of my jeep was a fellow from Boone County, North Carolina named Reece. We called him "Boone." He was 41 years old, about 5' 1", and illiterate. I read his mail for him, and taught him to sign his name, so he could sign the payroll.

Boone saved my life one day in Germany. I stopped to patch up a young German soldier who had been shot in the stomach. When I turned away for a minute, the German aimed a pistol at me, but Boone got him first. That taught me a lesson; don't turn your back on any German.

We often moved our heavy guns off the road to let the infantry, tanks and red ball express get by us.

We entered a town that had been abandoned by the residents, and were looking around for anything useful. I was carrying a Browning automatic rifle, and I encountered a man in German uniform carrying a machine gun. He spoke good English, introducing himself as an American who had joined the German army because he had been in college in Germany when the war started, and wanted to do what his friends were doing. We briefly looked at each other, turned, and started walking away in the opposite direction without firing a shot.

I was in Austria when the war ended.

After the war, I went back to C. V. Hill for a while, but then I took advantage of the GI Bill to learn how to grind lenses with the American Optical Company. They didn't teach me much; I think they were just milking the government.

So I got a job at a rubber company, making asbestos bricks. This didn't work out, so in 1946 I re-enlisted in the Army. I was sent to Fort Sill, where I was an instructor in radio, field wire, and switchboards. I married my wife, Ruth, in 1949. She is ten years younger than I. We lived in a rented apartment over the garage next to the home of an old couple who treated us very nicely. In 1952, our son was born, and I received orders to the Far East for the Korean War. Ruth was soon pregnant again, and I told her that would make it possible for me to stay in the States with her. But she vetoed the idea, saying, "You're a professional; when they call you, you go." She returned home, and gave birth to a baby girl at Mercer Hospital in Trenton.

I shipped out from California, thinking I was headed for Korea, but I ended up with the 29th Infantry on Okinawa. I had been an anti-aircraft instructor at Fort Sill, and a former colleague there discovered me and arranged for my transfer to the 507th Anti-Aircraft Operations Detachment.

The following year my wife joined me on Okinawa. We lived in a nice apartment on the top of a hill, completely furnished, even down to wine and wine glasses.

One day she noticed a big lump on my neck. I was sent to the Air Force Hospital. The doctors decided that it was probably cancerous, and they would have to ship me out the next day, because there were no facilities there for that kind of surgery. I told them I couldn't leave my wife and two kids behind. So they postponed the move for three days, so the whole family could go together. Finally, they gave me three days to pack up, then flew us home in a Navy transport to Boston.

At the Murphy Army Hospital in Massachusetts, they removed half my thyroid gland. Later, at Valley Forge, they removed most of the other half.

One of my fellow patients on the plane, about 6'4" and of good build, had lost one of his buttocks, lopped off by a shell that cut through him without exploding. When we arrived in Honolulu, a Japanese-American nurse scolded him for being lazy. She thought he was kidding when he told her he had lost his butt. When he showed it to her, she apologized. As we were heading toward our plane for the flight home, she insisted on examining him again. He got up on his knees. She reached under there. "Well," she said, "You've still got your family jewels!" We laughed all the way to Frisco.

Four of us were together at Murphy Army Hospital. One was a Jewish fellow from Brooklyn, who was on a strict diet because his intestines had been damaged by a mortar shell. But with the help of a family member he would go AWOL down to Brooklyn and pig out on a lot of Jewish food. When he came back, he'd be nearly dead.

Another Korean veteran had leg wounds from a mortar shell. He could walk, though he had no feeling in his legs. I remember one night I smelled something, and discovered that his leg was up against a hot radiator and burning.

When I left the hospital, I was assigned to security at Fort Devins, Massachusetts. I was discharged in 1945 and re-enlisted in 1946. I retired in 1963, with 22 years of service.

In retirement, I was a volunteer with the Ambulance Squad for 21 years, retiring at the age of 75 because our squad's insurance company insisted that I should no longer drive the ambulance. That was the only job available to me, because all the other squad positions were filled with paramedics.

At the age of 83, I am still active every other weekend, when my wife and I take charge of my son's Mobile gas station on Levittown Parkway in Fairless Hills.

HARRY WILLIS

Harry Willis

I was born in Philadelphia on September 17, 1917. I attended and graduated from Northeast High School in Philadelphia in 1935. I was married in 1942.

I enlisted in the United States Marine Corps (Reserve) on September 16, 1940. I was stationed at the Philadelphia Navy Yard, and had to report for reserve duty once a month. On one occasion, I was sent to Cuba for a short tour of duty. Shortly after I completed a four-year tour of duty with the Marine Corps Reserves at the age of 25, I was drafted, and joined the Army on March 15, 1944. I was sent to some camp in the south for infantry training. Just before I was shipped overseas, while playing volleyball I broke my hand, requiring a cast. This took me out of the task force to go overseas. Lucky for me, because my Division crossed the English Channel on D-Day, June 6, 1944.

In December, when I had recovered enough, I was sent overseas to join my old outfit, the 150th Division. When the big battle occurred, our outfit landed in Italy, and kept advancing northward until we reached France. On January 11, 1945, my unit, the 157th Regiment of the 45th Division, became engaged in a heavy artillery battle in the town of Rieperswiller, Alsace Lorraine Province, France. The battle was so intense that I lost my hearing in both ears from the artillery noise. More than 150 Americans were killed, another 350 were wounded, but were evacuated safely. I was one of 420 captured by the Germans. We were told by our commanders to surrender, lay down our weapons and march with our hands up. They marched us to a cattle car on a train, and forced to stand shoulder to shoulder with no sanitary facilities, water or food. The train took us to one of the two Stalag POW camps.

On February 6, 1945, my

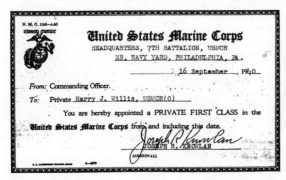

N. M. C. 1155—A.61

United States Marine Corps

HEADQUARTERS, 7TH BATTALION, USMCR

MB, NAVY YARD, PHILADELPHIA, PA.

16 September , 1940

From: Commanding Officer.

To: Private Harry J. Willis, USMCR(O)

You are hereby appointed a PRIVATE FIRST CLASS in the **United States Marine Corps** from and including this date.

JOSEPH R. KNOWLAN

(ORIGINAL)

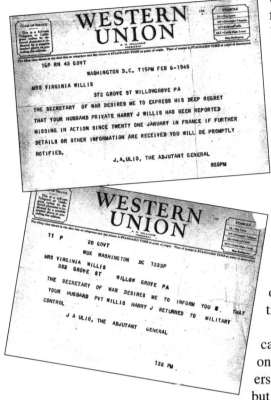

wife Virginia, received a message from the Adjutant General that I had been reported missing.

For five months, I wore the same clothing I had worn when I was captured. We were not able to take showers. We were fed rutabaga soup almost exclusively. We all suffered from malnutrition. I lost more than 50 pounds. Many of my comrades died, leaving those who were strong enough to remove their bodies. I made up my mind then and there that I was going to live; I wasn't going to give up.

We had to be aware of possible American stooges among the prisoners, who could monitor our activities and report to the Germans.

For most of the five months of captivity, I did nothing but sit. The only time the Germans had the prisoners go to work was to pick up bricks, but the prisoners were so undernourished and sick, that they could not pick up the assigned bricks. Some things you remember forever, some you can't, and don't want to.

The German guards had recruited certain prisoners to act as monitors of the rest of the men. For their efforts they were given warm clothing, good food, and the undying hatred of their fellow prisoners. When the war ended and the Stalags were liberated, the prisoners sought out their revenge on the cooperating Americans.

Liberation came on May 12, 1945, by troops led by British General Bernard Montgomery, Commander of the Eighth Army of the Allied Forces.

At the time of discharge, we were told that if we were considered a prisoner of war, we would be discharged immediately. Instead, when we arrived back in the States, they sent me to California for medical reasons. I had lost more than 50 pounds.

Before and after WW II, I attended both Temple and Drexel Universities. I never received a formal diploma, but I worked as a construction engineer on many interesting projects, including the Pennsylvania Turnpike bridge over the Delaware River, and the Chestnut and Market Street bridges in Philadelphia.

I was married in 1942 and have one daughter. My grandson is now serving in Iraq.

For service in WW II I was awarded three bronze stars for participation in the Rhineland Ardennes, Alsace, and Central Europe campaigns.

Some reminders of my experience in the war are:

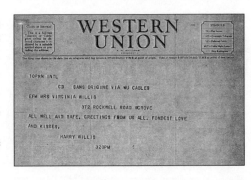

The Red Cross food package
Telegrams to my wife indicating my capture
My service in the Marine Corps
My service record, including awards.

AL YAMAMOTO

I was born in San Jose, California on October 29, 1925. My parents both came from Japan but I am an American, born of Japanese parents, sometimes referred to as Nisei. I graduated from high school in Gila River, Arizona, while in internment camp. At the time of the attack on Pearl Harbor, December 7, 1941, Helen (now my wife) and I both lived in California; we didn't know each other then. We met later, while attending high school, during internment in Arizona.

It was decided on the West Coast to evacuate all Japanese; the United States didn't want to take any chances. At one point, my family was ordered to sell

Al and Helen Yamamoto

what they could, and take what they could carry and meet for transportation to an undisclosed destination. Initially, we were subject to very primitive conditions until we arrived at a more permanent location in Arizona, where even then, there was only slight improvement. We were deported by train from California to Gila River, Arizona and interned for more than three years.

At one point, it became evident that the military was going to draft us. They were going to school me as an interpreter, but I washed out because I didn't know enough Japanese. I was still drafted and volunteered for the US Air Force. I was a company clerk, with the rank of first sergeant. However, by the time I was sent to a few camps in Kentucky and California, the war ended. We were discharged and returned home to our families. In leaving for home in California, I stopped by to see Helen in Monterrey. She was working for the Internal Revenue Service in San Francisco. We had been good friends in high school; I guess we knew then. I didn't propose to her..."We're going to be together," I said. But anyway, I was going to be discharged, so I said, "Okay, let's go home together." We were married in Oakland, in a Catholic Church, while I was still in my military uniform.

After the war, my father and mother came back east to find work in the Philadelphia area, and ended up in Newtown. My father, George Yamamoto, found out that Herman Heston, a local farmer, was looking for someone to work on his farm in 1946; my family has been here ever since. I was one of three sons; Kinzo, Tetsuo (Ted), and me, Al. I farmed in Newtown all my life. Originally it was my father's farm, and for a while I shared it with my brother, Ted. I owned and operated a greenhouse, and was best known for the produce and flowers from my 100 acre farm. I sold them at my roadside market on route 532, just outside of Newtown.

Ayao "Al" Yamamoto

October 29, 1925 - December 17, 2004

Years later, the Government under President Reagan's Administration signed legislation that apologized to some 120,000 Japanese-Americans who were forcibly interned in World War II. There was an award of $20,000, tax free, to be given to each eligible internee or designated beneficiary from a $1.2 billion trust fund created to pay reparation over a 10-year period.

I was a long-time member of the Rotary Club in Newtown, and a life-time member of the National Rifle Association. I have been an avid big game hunter, and enjoy salt water fishing on the North Carolina coast with hand-made rods made by my brother Kinzo.

My wife and I raised four children, three girls and a boy here on the farm in Newtown. The children attended all the local schools from first to twelfth grade.

Compiler's Note:
Al died in December 2004.

PETE CHESNER

I was born on May 8, 1913 in Newark, New Jersey, and moved to Newtown where I attended the Chancellor Street School until I graduated in 1930. I attended Penn State for a couple of years, because I was interested in medicine and wanted to become an eye doctor, an ophthalmologist. After two years I decided to come back to Newtown to work and live.

My introduction to WW II was when I received a draft notice. I was told to report to Philadelphia for a physical examination. They lined me up

Anne and Pete Chesner

against a wall along with a lot of other guys, put a card over my eye, which happened to be my good eye, and the guy looked at me and said, "What the hell are you doing here? Get out of here. We don't need you." So, that's how it happened. I had lost an eye in an accident, and so I only had one eye. I was immediately classified as 4-F. Later I was reclassified for limited service, and they assigned me to the US Air Force.

My first job was in Harrisburg, Pennsylvania with the First Air Cargo Resupply Squadron.

This made me very happy, because I wanted to do something for the war effort. They sent me to Burma to work in the Air Transport Command on the Air Lift, supplying food, supplies, and munitions to our troops and the Chinese.

We left Miami for Brazil on November 11, 1944, then across to Ascension Island, Khartoum, Aden, Karachi, Agra and then Laidu, ending up in Warazup, Burma on November 21, 1944.

We had no formal military training. After we arrived at our destination in India, they just put us out in the jungles, and opened up a runway for our airplanes to land and take off. Sometimes on either side of the runway there would be a dropoff of 10 to 12 feet, often full of water. We were called "Kickers." We would load our C-47 with supplies and take them to drop locations and virtually kick out the door the items to be dropped. We did what they call air drops.

Sometimes we would be visited by big brass. On one occasion, I think it was Lord Louis Mountbattan.

Our missions sometimes were as long as three hours. Our drops could be by parachute, or just kicked out the door. We flew more than 100 combat missions to resupply the fighting Chinese in Burma with medical supplies, food, and munitions. For this we received two Distinguished Flying Crosses. We flew with troops over the Himalayas, which we called the "HUMP." At all other times we resupplied our troops, or the Chinese, with food, medical supplies, and munitions.

Another aircraft used in transporting supplies and troops was the C-46. I took great pride in telling my fellow workers that the tail assembly was made in Newtown. They were so tired of me mentioning it that they threatened to kick me out on the next drop.

After the war, my wife and I owned and operated the White Hall Hotel for 35 years.

I was a charter member of the Rotary Club of Newtown and was elected Rotarian of the year in 1987. In the 1970s, I helped plan and plant Bradford pear trees along State Street in Newtown. In the Spring, when they are in bloom, they are a magnificent sight.

As a result of my experience in the Army Air Force in WW II, I helped establish the Bucks County Airport Authority.

Compiler's note:

Pete died on January 19, 2005 and his wife preceded him in death by less than a year.

CHARLIE CLAPPISON

I was born on September 27, 1922, in Cincinnati, where my father worked for the Square D Company. When he was transferred to their head office in Detroit, we moved to Birmingham, Michigan, about 18 miles from Detroit.

At the age of 14, when my mother died, my father sent me to military school because he had to go to work. I was at the Howe Military School, in Howe, Indiana, graduating with a US Army Reserve commission as 2nd lieutenant, which I had earned through ROTC training that included a

Charlie and Laura Clappison

summer at Fort Knox. I had hoped to go to the Naval Academy at Annapolis, but had to settle for the next best thing, a roundabout process that would send me to sea with the fleet in the Pacific, whence I would work my way to Norfolk, where I would be eligible, after further training, to apply to Annapolis.

I served nine months of sea duty on a destroyer, the *USS McDougal*. I passed the exam, and ended up in Norfolk. On the way, we found ourselves in Gander, Newfoundland, where we had the privilege of ferrying President Roosevelt from the cruiser *Augusta* to the battleship *King George*, where Churchill awaited him. A picture of me, standing by the rail, made it into *Life Magazine*.

In Norfolk, where I went in November, I passed the written exam for the Naval Academy, but flunked the eye exam. My father stepped in, and persuaded our congressman to arrange for my transfer to the Army, in which I already had an officer's commission. I went to an amphibious training center at Camp Edwards, Massachusetts. It was soon decided that in the winter we should be training in the south, so we went to Carrabelle, Florida, on the Gulf Coast, west of Tallahassee, to a facility specially built for amphibious training and the landing of LCIs. Infantry units came down, and we would run them through a training drill to make a beach landing and unload the ship.

We were picked for service in the Pacific. Early in 1945, we were in Hawaii preparing for the assault on Iwo Jima and working with the Marines. During one of the landings, we bent a propeller, and were dropped from the assault force. We remained on Oahu. By coincidence, we pitched our tents in fields near a sugar mill that I remembered visiting in 1940. We did no more amphibious training.

In fact, when we went ashore on Guam, the Philippines (Leyte and Ormoc), and Okinawa, we were not in the first echelon, and were not subject to enemy fire. In the assault on Okinawa, the platoon I commanded was part of a landing force that made a feint toward the southern part of the island, then made its landing near the middle. We relieved marine units that had made the original assault.

It was there, early one morning, that I lost my left leg, when a Japanese grenade rolled into the foxhole I occupied with two others. The medics quickly applied a tourniquet and got me to an aid station, so I survived. Of the 36-40 men in my platoon, we lost about 20, primarily to sniper fire. The snipers were positioned in the crowns of palm trees. They tied themselves to the trees, so they wouldn't fall out even when you killed them.

I was taken to a hospital ship called the *Hope,* where there were a lot of burn victims. We were told that the Navy suffered more casualties in the first month of the Okinawa campaign than either the Marines or the Army. My platoon sergeant told me later that new recruits were being killed before he could even learn their names.

From the hospital ship I was put in a hospital in Honolulu, where they amputated my leg. The next stop was Richmond, Virginia, where I was trained in the use of an artificial leg.

On June 17, 1943, I had married my wife, Laura. Our first child was born when I was on Guam. The Red Cross brought me the news.

I went to college under the GI Bill of Rights, attending the Wharton School at the University of Pennsylvania, near the home of my wife's family, the Cadwalladers of Yardley. By going to summer school, I was able to complete four years in three. I joined John Heinz and Company, a firm of certified public accountants, hoping to move eventually to the job of controller for one of our clients. I was able to do that at the Heineman Electric Company in Trenton, where after 27 years I retired as Treasurer.

A woodworking hobby led to an interest in clocks, for people often brought me small clocks to refinish. Because they looked miserable, I was able to buy them cheaply and refinish them. Then I would often repair the movement. I work once a week at the clock shop in Newtown, and also repair peoples' clocks here at Pennswood Village. Other hobbies are collecting stamps and slide rules.

My military service was the greatest maturing experience I could have had, with more responsibility then than any time in later life.

ARNETT CLARK

I was born November 23, 1922, at Washington Crossing, Pennsylvania, where I went to school through 8th grade. There was no bus transportation in those days. The nearest schools beyond 8th grade were in Yardley, New Hope or Newtown. I came to Newtown, but when I became 16, I quit school. I went to work for Lavelle Aircraft. At the age of 18, I was drafted by the Army in the fall of 1942. I was called to active duty in January 1943. I was sent to Ft. McClellan, Alabama, for basic training and infantry training. I also trained for six weeks conducting demolition work.

Arnett and Helen Clark

After my demolition training, we shipped out of New York for the South Pacific. We went through the Panama Canal, and then headed for Australia. We were on the ship for 40 days and 40 nights, zig-zagging all the way. We were escorted by destroyers until we arrived in Australia. We were there only a couple of days, and didn't get off the ship. There we were transferred to smaller ships that took us to New Guinea.

We arrived at Port Moresby, New Guinea, at nighttime. Port Moresby, New Guinea is not much more than 100 miles from Australia. It was the first place in New Guinea that the Allied Powers took back from the Japanese. We were taken ashore on barges, and put up in tents. The next morning, they gave us a treat of fresh eggs, anyway we wanted them. It was the first and last time we had any breakfast that suited us. Little did I know this was going to be my home for the next 30 months. A short time later, I was transferred to a boat battalion outfit at Milne Bay. We helped dock ships and worked with the longshoremen to help unload ships.

Later, I was assigned to, and lived on, a 72-foot tug. We traveled up and down the north coast of New Guinea, delivering food and supplies to the isolated ports of Finschafen, and Hollandia. Another job was to move some 300 bodies from the burial ground at Miline Bay to Finschafen. Here I am, an army man, trained in the infantry, and specialized training in demolition, doing Navy work. After almost 30 months, they moved me to the Philippines for more Navy work, splicing rope and cables, and teaching others to do the same.

I was only in the Philippines a short time, and then the war ended. I boarded a ship for the long trip back to San Francisco. How good it was to see the Golden

Arnett Clark

Gate Bridge. After a few days in San Francisco, we boarded a train for the East Coast. I was discharged from the Army in January of 1946 at Indiantown Gap, Pennsylvania. I served exactly three years in the military during World War II. For a while, I did a few odd jobs, and then went to work with Teschner, a painting contractor.

I met Helen Kumeiga within a few months after I came home. We were married a year and a half later. We lived with my parents on Liberty Street in Newtown for a short time, and then bought a place on South Lincoln Avenue, and lived there for 10 years. I married Helen Kumiega June 14, 1947. We have two children, a boy and a girl, five grandchildren and one great-grandchild. I learned the trade of carpentry, and eventually ended up specializing in making cabinets.

In 1958 I bought a lot on Frost Lane in Newtown, and built my own house. After almost 50 years, I live at the same place.

The last 14 years, before my retirement, I spent as a building inspector for both Newtown Borough and Newtown Township.

I retired in 1987, and still do odd jobs, but most of all I enjoy my winters in Florida with my wife, playing golf, eating potluck suppers, and playing my mandolin with several small groups, that play old-time and country music. I have enjoyed my retirement. So far, my wife and I have spent 18 consecutive winters in Florida.

Arnett (kneeling on left) with some of his buddies.

BILL CRAIGHEAD

Bill Craighead

I was born on August 20, 1925, in Gettysburg, Pennsylvania, and grew up in Harrisburg, Pennsylvania. I graduated from George School, a Quaker preparatory school in Newtown, Pennsylvania, in February, 1944. I was drafted on March 11, 1944 and I chose to serve in the Navy. My boot camp training was at Great Lakes Naval Training Station, North Chicago, Illinois. After only three and a half weeks of boot camp, I was sent to Little Creek, Virginia for three months of Amphibious Training. During that time, I was assigned to a ship's crew that was the first to man the *USS LSM 215* in Philadelphia, Pennsylvania on July 23, 1944.

After a week of becoming familiar with our duties aboard ship, and taking on supplies, we left Philadelphia and headed back to Little Creek, Virginia for a two-week shakedown cruise on the Chesapeake Bay. The batteships *Wisconsin*, and *Missouri* had just recently been commissioned, and were on their shakedown cruises also. It gave us a feeling of confidence and even security just to see them. Little did we realize then that they would appear eight months later at Okinawa in support of our landing craft, while unloading five medium Sherman tanks and the crews to operate them.

Finally, after another two weeks of training, on August 30, 1944 we left Norfolk, Virginia for the Pacific via the Panama Canal, with a new Captain. As it turned out, he was the second of eight Captains we had during our 21 months of service.

We spent two months on the California Coast at San Diego and San Francisco. Some of our time was spent conducting landings and gunnery practice on or near San Clemente Island, just off the California coast.

Not all our time was spent on military maneuvers and preparing our ship for sea. During our two months in San Diego, most of the crew were able to visit Hollywood, and enjoy the Hollywood Canteen before leaving the States. In the week we spent in the San Francisco Bay area, we loaded our well-deck with pilings at the docks in Oakland to take to Pearl Harbor. Once again, we had enough free time to enjoy the many sights of San Francisco, which most of us had never seen before. We went to movies, dined in fine restaurants, enjoyed the entertainment at the night clubs, and restaurants on Fisherman's Wharf.

Bill Craighead

Leaving San Francisco was exciting. Crossing the Bay area from Oakland, we passed by Alcatraz, and then under the Golden Gate Bridge, leaving Oakland and San Francisco behind us. After the war, many of us thought: "The Golden Gate in '48 and back alive in '45."

It was an eight-day trip to Pearl Harbor. Arriving there on November 25, 1944, we spent most of our time in the Hawaiian Islands preparing for an invasion (Iwo Jima). While there, we spent time conducting landings, and in anti-aircraft gunnery practice. In early January 1945, we took on board five medium Sherman tanks with Marine Corps crews to operate them. We spent several more days conducting practice landings at Hilo, Hawaii. Then it was time to join the task force for the invasion of Iwo Jima. We were on our way back to Pearl Harbor to join the task force, when our Captain reported to the Fleet Commander a bad vibration aboard ship. As it turned out, this problem took us out of the invasion force. What a disappointment this was to most of the crew. It resulted in a change in command and the unloading of our tanks and crew to another landing craft. We now had our fourth Captain. This one remained aboard for ten months, and took us through the Okinawa campaign.

It turned out that we had a bent screw (propeller) from all the practice landings. We had to go into dry-dock for repairs, but after a month we were on our way again. This time we were headed for Guam, and then on to the Philippines. We were at sea for about a month. After three weeks in the Philippines, we joined the task force for the invasion of Okinawa, "Operation Iceberg." We left Leyte March 25, 1945 and arrived on D-Day, April 1, 1945, Easter Sunday. The invasion armada of ships was an awesome sight. There were ships of all kinds as far as the eye could see. The seas were very rough for most of the five days, and practically all of the tank crews were seasick the entire trip. Some of the tank crews were known to have said that they would rather be fighting on the beaches than experiencing seasickness. About 12 hours before the landings however, the seas around Okinawa became as calm as glass. This enabled most of the tank crews to recover for the landing. The fact that the tank crews and infantry were unopposed was extremely important to the health and condition of the landing forces. By the time we arrived in the vicinity of Okinawa on D-Day, there were 800 ships of all kinds. All of our battleships were there, 14 in all, pounding the beaches with their 14 and 16 inch guns.

We put ashore five medium Sherman tanks on the beach named Purple II, just off Yontan airfield. On 23 of the 25 days we were at Okinawa, we were subject to kamikaze attacks by suicide aircraft. On April 6th we were under continual air attacks for 22 hours. It seemed as if there were as many as 100 kamikazes shot down in one day in the vicinity of our ships. Day after day we unloaded ships and took supplies and troops into the beach. After 25 days, we were sent to Saipan for a little R&R (rest and recreation), before heading south to Guadalcanal to pick up spare airplane parts and return to Guam.

We crossed the equator on July 3, 1945, at longitude 136° 52' and latitude 00° 00' 00", and celebrated it in true naval tradition.

It was on our return trip from Guadalcanal, while at sea, July 30, 1945 in the same general area as the *Indianapolis* when she was torpedoed. While we were still at sea, the first atomic bomb was dropped on Hiroshima, August 6, 1945. We arrived on Guam August 9, 1945, as the second atomic bomb was dropped on Nagasaki.

August 14, 1945 was V-J Day, the end of WW II, and a great relief for all of us. The war however, would not end for us. Within a few weeks, we found ourselves on our way to China to take occupation troops and food supplies to Tientsin, China and return Japanese troops back to Japan.

Now that the war was over we found ourselves even further away from home, almost 10,000 miles from New York City.

We left China in the middle of October. It was a slow but steady trip back to the States. Leaving Guam was quite an adventure. Our captain was eligible for discharge so he left the ship at Guam and was replaced by our fifth captain who proceeded to run us aground as we were leaving Apra Harbor, Guam. We were fully loaded with extra troops, and our homeward bound pennant, 88 feet in length, was flying high, a foot long for every man aboard who had been overseas at least a year, including the passengers.

At high tide the next day, we were able to get back to sea again. We had enough fuel aboard to get back to the States, but our ship had developed severe leaks, which meant we not only steadily lost fuel, but we had leaks in our crew's quarters, and aft steering compartments that had to be pumped out day and night. We were fortunate to have enough fuel to make it to Pearl Harbor. We laid over at Pearl Harbor a week for repairs, and then headed for San Diego, arriving State-side on December 21, 1945.

At this point, we were anxious to get back to sea again, and get home. I suddenly realized that most of my time at sea was in the pilot house as a radar operator, and/or helmsman. In fact, I had steered a ship many more miles than I had driven a car at the time of my discharge. When I arrived back in the States,

I expected to obtain leave. Only those that had accumulated enough points were eligible for discharge, and could leave the ship. The rest of us had to stay aboard for four more months to help decommission the ship.

My time spent aboard ship during the decommissioning process was very unpleasant. I had just spent 13 months in the Pacific, including the first 30 days of the Okinawa campaign, and couldn't get any leave. Because I didn't have enough points for discharge, I had to stay aboard ship and prepare her for decommissioning. To even paint the ship at this point was absolutely unnecessary, since it would just be sold as scrap. We had no cooks and lived like dogs. Just before decommissioning, the captain gave me the ship's Bible and I was able to finagle a way to get the ship's bell.

When the day came to leave the ship, I was one of two of the original crew of 48 that both commissioned and decommissioned the ship. I was what the Navy called a "plank owner," one who commissioned a ship. The final day came on April 17, 1946. I left San Diego on a 30-day leave and headed for home, being discharged on June 2, 1946.

I had a pleasant summer at home with the neighborhood gang, seeing many of my high school classmates before entering Gettysburg College in the fall.

I obtained an A.B. degree under the GI Bill from Lebanon Valley College in 1952, and an M.S. in zoology from Pennsylvania State University in 1965.

I married Betty Bakley in 1953. We have a son, now married. One older son died in 1993 and is survived by his wife and two daughters, Katy and Sarah.

I taught biology at George School for fifteen years. I also worked for more than ten years with State and Federal agencies, developing effluent standards for industry and water quality standards for the Delaware River Basin. I spent several years working with a private utility in New Jersey, conducting ecological studies for the siting of nuclear power plants.

For 30 years, I have worked with honeybees in Pennsylvania and Florida.

As a volunteer, I have worked part-time for the Florida Marine Research Institute, assisting in a program to restore the queen conch to the Florida Keys.

JOHN AND FRANK CRAIGHEAD

Frank and I were identical twins born on August 14, 1916 in Washington D.C., to Frank and Carolyne Craighead. We graduated from Western High School in Washington, D.C., in 1933, and then attended Pennsylvania State University, graduating Phi Beta Kappa in 1937. As avid Boy Scouts, we received our Eagle Scout badges at the age of sixteen.

Our early interest in nature and the out-of-doors came from our father, a PhD entomologist with the US Department of Agriculture in Washington D.C.. His two brothers, Charles and Eugene, also encouraged our love of nature and our skills as outdoor men.

Our service story really begins in Ann Arbor, Michigan, where Frank and I were working towards our doctorate degrees in the Department of Forestry and Conservation. As part of an assistantship, and in conjunction with the University and the Department of Defense, we established a program of physical conditioning to teach students out-of-doors activity skills. We subjected our students to cross-country courses using compass and map, hiking through bogs, canoeing, rappelling, tree climbing, and the like. We often ended each class around a fire, cooking steaks or meatballs and roasting corn gleaned from nearby fields. On alternate days we met in the gym for wrestling. The popularity of

Frank

John

our course was due in large part to the many young men wanting to get a 'leg up' on their training, in anticipation of induction into the Armed Services.

Our own academic deferment was coming to an end. Unable to sell the military on the idea of expanding a civilian physical training program, we enlisted in the Mountain Troops, assuring ourselves that we would at least train and fight in an environment we loved. Mountaineering friends of ours, Jack Durance and Capt. Robert Bates, were already a part of this unit, and they assured us that we would have a good chance of being accepted. It was a huge relief to have our service commitment finally settled. The uncertainty of planning a future in wartime was wearing.

Frank and I were enjoying our last weeks at college when life again went topsy-turvy. A Lieutenant in the Navy called, asking if we would accept a commission in the Navy, as our outdoor training program was just what they wanted. The University of Michigan ROTC unit wanted to delay our induction so Frank and I could instruct their instructors in Judo, wrestling, and woodcraft, in order to continue the P. E. course. Then the Army called us telling us to forget the Navy offer because they were hatching a plan of their own. To top it all off, Frank was given a deferment, and I was instructed to report.

By the time everything was sorted out, Frank and I found ourselves as Naval lieutenants attached to the physical training department. We were charged with developing a pre-flight course and curriculum for providing Naval aviators with physical hardening and survival skills. Our first task was to create a training manual and then to set up the program at various training centers. The long hours of study and writing required at the University were turned directly to this new task. At our station in Chapel Hill, we soon acquired the nickname of "the Beavers." Our manual, "How to Survive on Land and Sea," was published, and we then set up training at flight stations in Texas, Florida, South Carolina, California, Panama, Brazil, the Galapagos, and other flight schools.

Captain Hamilton, our immediate superior, had taken a personal interest in our work, believing it to be very important. He returned our ship assignment requests with the assurance that we would get overseas as soon as our work with the training programs was finished. When the war ended, we were still at it. To honor his promise, Capt. Hamilton issued us, arguably, the Navy's best ever overseas orders. We were to go and collect, first hand, additional information on survival techniques in the Pacific, for a revised edition of the survival book. We were given a free hand to request transportation, and supplies at all Navy bases.

With this purpose, Frank and I visited many of the Pacific islands, learning woodcraft and subsistence techniques from the natives. In the Marshall Islands, we were dropped on a small atoll, with a native guide, Goneske, where we lived off the bounty of a Pacific island, and learned the subsistence lore of his people. In the Philippines, we had a small Negrito guide, Antonio. Antonio was barely four feet tall, but a tireless jungle trekker. He carried a bow with three arrows, which he never lost. He brought down monkeys with it for the stew pot. Gulam taught us the behavior of the jungle cock, and how to fool him into showing himself to our weapons. He also introduced us to new forms of matchless fire making.

Everywhere in the Pacific, we found the peoples friendly and eager to share their lifestyles. Before leaving the Pacific, we were stationed briefly in Japan, where Frank and I witnessed the destructive power of the Atomic bomb and found time to make a winter ascent of Mt. Fuji.

During this time Frank and I tried to get our cousin, Bill Craighead, assigned to us. Bill was also in the Navy, assigned to LSM 215. Our miraculous orders were apparently not good enough to free him from his shipboard assignment.

As idyllic as this time might seem, Frank and I encountered obstacles. We contracted "back break fever", an ailment similar to malaria and carried by mosquitos. Homesickness threatened to turn a lifetime adventure into drudgery. Both Frank and I had married during the war, Frank to Ester Stevens, a perky blond he met at the University of Michigan. She was from Evanston, Illinois. I married Margaret Smith, a brunette from Ogden, Utah. We met Margaret while climbing in the Grand Tetons of Wyoming. Thoughts of our wives and civilian life beckoned, but before we could return home to our wives and civilian life, a revision of the survival manual still had to be completed, incorporating knowledge and survival techniques we had learned and used in the Pacific.

Frank and I were discharged on March 20, 1946. We were awarded the following Navy Commendation by the Secretary of the Navy, James Forrestal.

The Citation:

" For outstanding performance of duty as an acknowledged authority in the field of survival in the Survival Training Program for the Physical and Military Training Section of the Aviation Training Division, DCNO (Air), of the United States Navy, from December 28, 1942 to March 20, 1946. A skilled writer, lecturer and scientific expert in Forestry, conservation and wildlife, Lieutenant Craighead delved into the obscure field of survival, leading an expedition through the Western Pacific and Japan and taking field survival classes on actual tropical trips, with his identical twin brother, to gather data, in order to communicate this knowledge of how to live on land and sea to naval aviators and air crewmen. Since up to that time there was no organized material available on survival, Lieutenant Craighead and his brother prepared the material for their book, "How to Survive on Land and Sea," which now is widely used by other branches of the service and Allied Nations. In traveling from air station to air station, he skillfully set up and coordinated the survival training programs and instructed other officers to carry it out. By his uncanny native ingenuity, Lieutenant Craighead devised new techniques of building shelters, methods of catching game and skills for living off the land and sea. His devotion to duty was in keeping with the highest traditions of the United States Naval Service."

Frank was awarded the same commendation. Shortly after the war, Frank and

I were asked by the Strategic Air Command to set up a survival training program for the B-29 pilots and other forces. This time, the training was to be devised for Northern Temperate climes. Frank and I, unwilling to re-enlist, agreed to do it, but only as civilian consultants.

We were eventually able to pursue our scientific and academic interests. In 1958 we received our doctorates from the University of Michigan Forestry department, in Bio-Ecology. Our work since, in wildlife ecology and conservation, has brought many awards. Among them was the 1988 National Geographic Society Centennial Award which included among its recipients such well known figures as Jacques-Yves Cousteau, Sir Edmund Hillary, the Leakeys, Dr. Robert Ballard, John Glenn, Dr. Jane Goodall, Thayer Soule and others.

I now live in Missoula, Montana. My brother Frank died October 21, 2001. A Craighead Chair in Wildlife Biology has recently been endowed at the University of Montana in recognition of the Craigheads' lifelong work.

BOB DILKS

I was born September 9, 1917 in Philadelphia, Pennsylvania. I went to school in Bensalem, but never graduated from high school. I was drafted, along with my brother, on February 4, 1942.

I reported for duty in Bristol, Bucks County, Pennsylvania. We boarded a train to Fort Meade, and then were shipped to Macon, Georgia for six months of preliminary training. Then we were shipped to a place called Oyster, Virginia, for four or five months. I was trained in the infantry as a rifleman. I was assigned to the 111th infantry, and then went to Camp Pendleton, California for shipment overseas.

Our infantry group was split up and sent to different places. I was part

Bob Dilks

of a group that boarded a ship for Pearl Harbor, Hawaii. We had further training there in preparation for the invasion of Kwajalein, February 8, 1944. When Kwajalein was secured, we were sent back to Hawaii again for a little rest and recreation, and further training. In October 1945 we were sent to Peleliu as occupation forces, and that is where we stayed for the rest of the war. This was a bad campaign for the American forces, for we had heavy losses at Peleliu. My time there was spent as a cook, rising to the rank of sergeant.

One day I was using a device called a salamander to heat hot water. When I lit it, it exploded, and I was hospitalized for two months with skin burns. After many shots, my burns cleared up on my arm and the side of my face. Then I was sent back to the States.

I went back to Texas by airplane, and then to Maryland. We were discharged immediately, on the 13th of December 1945. I served in the Army almost four years, from February 2, 1942 to December 13, 1945.

My wife picked me up at the Langhorne train station. We were married in 1943, when I had a 10-day furlough, on the farm in Ivyland. I've been married 62 years. My wife, who worked many years as a schoolteacher, is still alive. I'm 88 years old. We had four children, nine grandchildren, and one great grandchild.

When I came home, I went to work for the oil company where I worked before the war. In 1952, I decided to go into business on my own. I was delivering oil and gas to the local farmers, and have been in the oil business here in Newtown ever since. Along with one of my sons, I still remain active in my oil business.

JACK DISHAW

I was born on July 26, 1926 in Ogdens-burg, New York. I left high school at the end of my junior year to join the U.S. Navy for three years, or the duration of World War II.

I joined the Navy in 1943, at the age of 17. After boot training at Sampson, New York and gunnery and seaman-ship school in Newport, Rhode Island, I was assigned to the *USS Alaska*, a battle cruiser, the first of its kind (but the third American naval vessel to bear the name), then being built at the Philadelphia Navy Yard. I was sent to the Navy Yard before the ship was completed. When it was finished, I took up my duties aboard, as a Storekeeper Third Class, one of about 2,000 shipmates.

Jack Dishaw

My battle station was in the lower handling room for a 5-inch gun mount.

On August 6, 1944, the Alaska headed down the Delaware River, bound for Hampton Roads, Virginia, escorted by the Simpson DD221 and the Boom DD210. An extensive shakedown cruise took us to Annapolis on the Chesapeake Bay, and then down to the Gulf of Perea, off Trinidad. On the return journey to Philadelphia, we stopped in Norfolk, and again in Annapolis. At the Philadelphia Navy Yard, there were alterations to our fire control suite, and the fitting of four MK57 directors for 5-inch batteries.

Battle cruisers were known as CBs. Alaska was CB1, Guam was CB2, and CB3 was named Hawaii, but it was never finished.

We left Philadelphia on November 12, 1944, sailed to Guantanamo Bay, passed through the Panama Canal on December 2, and arrived at San Diego on December 12. There we were trained in on-shore bombardment and anti-aircraft fire. We moved on to San Francisco on January 8, and then on to Pearl Harbor on January 13. On January 27, our commanding officer, Captain Fischler, was pro-moted to flag rank, and was succeeded by Captain Kenneth M. Noble.

We left Pearl Harbor on January 29, and on February 10, 1945 we joined Task Group 58.4, part of the famous Task Force 58, known as the Fast Carrier Task Force. On February 10, our task group sailed for the Japanese home islands, with the mission of screening the aircraft carriers as they carried out night air strikes against Tokyo and its airfields. Almost three-quarters of the men had never seen action before, and sought out the veterans in their midst for counsel and advice.

Leaving the Philippines, we went on to the invasion of Iwo Jima, where for about a month our sole function was taking part in the bombardment. We could hardly see the island. We didn't experience attacks from suicide bombers until the assault on Okinawa, of which we were a part from Day One. There we were part of a group of ships with the mission of protecting the four aircraft carriers *Yorktown*, *Intrepid*, *Independence*, and *Langley*, against both air and surface attacks. The Task Force left Ulithi in the Carolines on March 15, refueled at sea on the following day, and reached a point southeast of Kyushu early on March 18. From there, our planes joined with those of Task Groups 58.1, 58.2, and 58.3 in bombarding Japanese airfields at Usaoita and Saiki.

We claimed 170 enemy aircraft destroyed on the ground and another 77 engaged over the target area. The Japanese retaliated. Thanks to poor weather, our radar provided little if any warning.

We spotted a Francis, a suicide bomber headed toward the stern of the nearby Intrepid. Alaska's guns exploded it into fragments with a direct hit. I saw it all from my watch station as a J-A talker on the bridge. My job was to get from our air lookouts information on the location of enemy aircraft and relay it to the Captain, or other officer in charge. On this occasion, I alerted the captain to the suicide bomber as it headed for the carrier, and we watched while one of our gunners blew it out of the sky with a 5-inch gun.

Suicide attacks continued for the rest of the day. Gunfire from our ships downed almost two dozen planes, while our aircraft downed about a dozen others. Alaska was responsible for a second enemy bomber.

The next morning, one of our photo reconnaissance aircraft discovered a large number of major Japanese fleet units in the Inland Sea. Our aircraft engaged targets of opportunity over Kobe, Hiroshima, and Kuri. The attacks were only moderately successful, thanks to extremely heavy and accurate enemy anti-aircraft fire. Japanese aircraft also counter-attacked, hitting our Task Group 58.2, which lay some 20 miles north of the other Groups in Task Force 58.

At about 07:08, the *USS Franklin*, an aircraft carrier (CB-13), took two bomb hits, and our CB-18 also fell victim to Japanese bombs.

With our radar largely useless, Japanese planes attacked all our Task Groups. During the afternoon, Task Force 58 retired slowly to the southwest, covering the crippled *Franklin* and simultaneously launching fire sweeps against airfields on Kyushu in order to disorganize any strike against it. A salvage unit, which we called Task Unit 58.29, was formed. It was composed of the *Alaska*, her sister ship the *Guam*, four aircraft carriers, the heavy cruisers *Pittsburgh* and *Santa Fe*, and three destroyer divisions. Our mission was to screen the damage to "Big Ben," as her crew affectionately called her, so she could travel at her best speed toward Guam.

Things went well that morning, but in the afternoon what we thought were Japanese aircraft appeared. We soon identified the first one as one of our own aircraft. That caught us off guard, so we were surprised when the second one turned out to be Japanese. Only its poor marksmanship saved the Franklin from another bomb hit. Our gunfire at the plane wasn't much more accurate, so it escaped unscathed. The only casualties on the *Alaska* were men burned by splashes from our own mount 51. Later in the day, 15 men hurt on the *Franklin* received medical treatment on the *Alaska*.

Not long thereafter, the *Franklin* headed back to Pearl Harbor, towed by the Santa Fe, and we returned to the war.

In anticipation of the battle of Okinawa, beginning on Easter Sunday, April 1, 1944, we joined on March 27 a task group that included us as well as *Guam* (a sister ship), *San Diego Flint*, and *Destroyer Squadron 47*. Our mission was to carry out the bombardment of a small island 160 miles east of Okinawa. No answering fire came from the beach, and our observers noted satisfactory firing on the island.

When the battle for Okinawa began, we resumed our mission of screening the fast carriers as they supported the invasion.

USS Alaska CB-1

June 17, 1944	Commissioned Philadelphia, Pennsylvania
August 6, 1944	Shakedown cruise Chesapeake Bay
December 13, 1945	Westward Passage through the Panama Canal
February 19, 1945	Iwo Jima
April 1, 1945 (Easter Sunday)	Okinawa
Mid-August 1945	War's end
July 16, 1945	China Operations
August 30, 1945	7th fleet occupation of Inchon, Korea
December 13, 1945	Eastward Passage through the Panama Canal
February 17, 1947	Decommissioned

The *Alaska* was awarded three battle stars during WW II

After the war I worked as an ironworker building bridges. I was married in 1954 and have two children. I married my second wife in 1961, and have lived in Newtown, Pennsylvania since 1965.

I like to go to ship reunions, which we still have every year. I enjoy playing golf and working with wood.

BEN EMGE

Ben Emge

I was born at home, delivered by a mid-wife, on December 21, 1920, in Belleville, Illinois. I graduated from high school in the class of 1938. On Pearl Harbor day, I was at the University of Illinois in Champaign-Urbana, participating in an ROTC cavalry unit. After talking to the Navy recruiters, I decided service at sea as a pilot was preferable to riding horseback. I took my physical exam in St. Louis, where Edna Mae, my wife, was living. I was assigned in the summer of 1942 to a pre-flight school at the University of Iowa, followed by flight training at Olathe, Kansas, where I became an ensign in May 1943. Edna Mae (also a Belleville native) and I were married on July 12, 1943. We are the parents of four daughters.

I was selected for dive-bombing, first with the Douglas Dauntless and then with the Curtis Hell Diver. In California, I joined Carrier Air Group 18, consisting of about 30 dive-bombers, 30 torpedo planes, and 40 fighters. I flew a dive-bomber.

We were moved to Hawaii, well after Pearl Harbor. In fact, there were no carriers in Pearl Harbor on December 7, 1941, a fortunate coincidence, for the carriers played an essential role later on. At Pearl Harbor, we participated in a competition among the three types of planes. We won the competition, only to discover that the prize was the opportunity to be the first to go to sea, on the carrier *Intrepid,* and engage the Japanese.

We were in the Western Pacific for six months. Our first encounter with the enemy was at Babeldaob, on Peleliu, in the Palau Islands. But our main strikes were in the Philippines and Formosa. In mid-November 1943, off the Philippines, we participated in the Battle of the Philippine Sea, where the Japanese fleet was decimated, with the help of dive bombers and torpedo planes. But we were also victims of kamikaze attacks, which cost us more than 90 lives.

In the battle of the Philippine Sea in mid-October 1944, I would like to quote from a book, Hell Divers. The author, John F. Forsyth, in his account of this mission to sink one of the two largest Japanese battleships, makes reference to Ben Emge. Forsyth had just dropped a bomb on the aft deck of the Musachi. A direct hit. In his get-away, "I saw no other airplanes. I felt like the only survivor; I didn't see how any plane could dive through the fire and come out. Then I saw other bombers and a few torpedo planes. They joined up gradually, until almost all were back in formation. It seemed incredible that so many could get through. True, they were holed and battered, but there they were. Don Freet and Ben Emge came back beside me. Ben's engine was smoking and cutting out for seconds every so often, but he worried it back across the Philippines and then out onto our haven, the broad Pacific, where American ships would find us if we went down into the water, and survived the crash. Miraculously, that tough Wright engine kept him in the air and brought him back to the ship."

On one occasion our cooks, all black men, were brought up from the galley to man anti-aircraft guns. At the time I was just returning to the carrier, and could see a kamikaze approaching. I made a split-second decision to land rather than turn away. The kamikaze struck the ship just after I caught the wire. I could feel the heat of the ensuing fire on the back of my neck. The Japanese plane wiped out nine cooks who were manning a gun on the port side of the ship. One of the survivors was belatedly awarded the Navy Cross by the Reagan administration.

Our ship was finally put out of action, so we returned to Pearl Harbor, and from there to the west coast. We were back in the States for Christmas.

I had eight years of active duty, including four years during the Korean War. When I returned home, I started a small company that produced safety and survival equipment, first in Trenton, and later in the Newtown Industrial Commons. I sold the business in 1979, and turned to the renovation of old buildings, such as the Brick and Whitehall Hotels. We are now retired and living in a cottage at Chandler Hall, in Newtown.

Compiler's Note:

Ben died in 2003 and was buried in Arlington National Cemetery in Virginia, with full military honors.

BILL ERRICO

I was born in Trenton, New Jersey in 1927, when my parents lived in Titusville. In the 10th grade, I got into an argument with a teacher. He smacked me in the face, and I knocked him down. They promoted me to the 11th grade, but I decided I had had enough school, so I joined the Navy. It was only recently that I received a high school diploma, thanks to Mike Donovan. I was only 16, so I changed the year of birth on my birth certificate from 1927 to 1925, and went down to Philadelphia and joined the Navy. I enlisted in 1944 and was discharged in 1948.

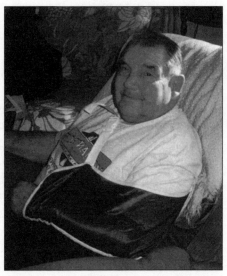

Bill Errico

I went to Great Lakes, Illinois for six weeks in boot camp, followed by a month and a half at a school for signalmen, and then on to San Francisco, where I was assigned to the *USS Stack*, a destroyer (DD406). I stayed there for about a year. But a signalman was needed on the *USS Grass* (ARS24), a salvage and rescue ship, which I joined in San Francisco. After Pearl Harbor we joined a Task Force of 800 ships—40 miles wide, 80 miles long—destined for the invasion of the Philippines. I remember encountering just one Japanese airplane, which took pictures of our entire task force without being fired on by any of our ships.

We took part in the battle of the Philippine Sea in late October 1944. After the first big invasion of the Philippines, we went on to Corregidor and Bataan, where we lost several ships and a lot of sailors. One of them was an LSM, a landing ship medium. After our men had removed their life jackets to prepare for the landing, the LSM hit a mine. The half-track we were carrying was turned upside down. Pieces of human bodies were floating all over the place.

We went on to Manila, and found the harbor clogged by Japanese ships sitting on the bottom, with their decks still awash.

The invasion of Corregidor took care of everything. We picked up three Japanese soldiers who were trying to escape from Corregidor on a raft. They had rifles under their raft, but we took control of them and turned them over to intelligence.

Our next destination was Okinawa, where Bill Swayze, an Army man and a classmate of mine at Newtown High School, lost his life. I was on a salvage ship.

A big job for us there was to pull a big merchant ship off a coral reef that was only four feet under the surface of the ocean. It took us four or five days to do the job. The American fleet was under attack by Japanese suicide planes. Two of them attacked us, but missed. I believe I shot one of them down, for my tracers had gone right into his propeller. The other one killed a couple of our boys. We had to bury them at sea, doing our best to make a ceremony of it.

We sewed them into canvas and put a five-inch shell between their legs, so that they went to the bottom.

Among my souvenirs from that time are some .31-caliber Japanese slugs and a couple of .50-caliber slugs from our own airplanes.

At Subic Bay, we observed, at night, a tank battle between American and Japanese tanks. At a place called Zigzag Pass, we watched some American tanks chase a group of Japanese tanks, three of which careened into the ocean.

I also experienced a typhoon. At the time I was on the salvage ship Grass ARS-24. Three of our destroyers capsized, in ninety-foot waves.

When the war ended, I had enough points to return home. After 30 days at home in Newtown, I was called back to San Francisco for two weeks. But I arranged with the Commander of the Philadelphia Naval District to assign me to Philadelphia, where I served as a chauffeur, driving officers back and forth between the Philadelphia Navy Yard and 30th Street Station.

I was discharged from the Navy at Bainbridge, and came to live in Bucks County, first in Levittown, but mostly in Newtown. With my first wife I had three sons. When we divorced, I was granted custody of the boys. Later, in 1960, I married a wonderful girl, who raised those boys and the three boys and a girl that we had together. She died of diabetes in September 1999.

I am a carpenter by trade, starting off in a partnership with a family member, and thereafter working for every contractor in Newtown. We had good times together. I did things like additions, alterations, and rec rooms.

Hunting was a major interest. I would kill a deer every year, right outside Newtown. We enjoyed the venison.

HUMMEL FAGER

I was born July 13, 1926 in Harrisburg, Pennsylvania, graduated from high school in June 1944 and immediately enlisted in the Navy. After 12 weeks of boot camp training at Bainbridge, Maryland, I attended quartermasters school at the same facility. After the completion of quartermasters school, I was shipped to the West Coast to Shoemaker, California, an outgoing unit for the Pacific theater. We got in trucks and were driven to San Francisco, then went by boat to Treasure Island. The food was excellent, not exactly the navy chow that we were used to. We boarded the Matsonia, a ship of the Matson Line, that before the war had taken people to Hawaii.

Hummel Fager

The ship had WAVES on it. The first night out there was a storm, and I was a guard in the passageway, and there was a scuttlebutt in the passageway. The WAVES would come out to get a sip of water and pretty soon one of them threw up and then another. Soon I had "mal de mer."

Shortly after arriving at Pearl Harbor, we boarded another troop ship heading west. Later I was transferred to the Destroyer *Blue*, and from there to the *USS Vicksburg*, the light cruiser CL 86, by high-line.

The Vicksburg was in the bombardment fleet at Okinawa, among battleships, heavy and light cruisers, and destroyers. We would shell the Japanese positions all day and then go to the Nakagusuku Wan (Buckner Bay) and load ammunition. At night, we would sometimes shoot 5-inch star shells over the Jap positions. One day we fired 2,400 rounds of 5-inch and 6-inch shells in 6 hours. At Buckner Bay we would load shells every day, and sometimes anchor there at night. If Jap planes came over at night, we had an LCVP that was tied to our stern, make smoke to hide us. An ensign assigned to the mast-top said that one moonlight night the smoke only rose so high, and all the masts of the fleet were showing. On May 20th 1945, we were assigned to sink an American destroyer that had run aground on a shoal at Okinawa. The destroyer Longshaw had stuck itself on a reef, had been shelled by the Japs, and was abandoned as she was unable to spot Jap cannons. We sank her with 6-inch shells.

At Okinawa, we shelled Japanese shore installations during the day, and with 5-inch star shells, lit up the Jap lines at night. We ate and slept at odd times. One night, during the mid-watch, I had the wheel, and as nothing was going on, I went back to the radio shack and got a stool. The bridge, as usual, was blacked out, and since nobody could see I sat down. We were steaming at 3 knots, just fast enough to have steerage, and I fell sleep. When I woke up, I had turned the ship around, and I was going the wrong way. I turned the rudder over 15 degrees and did a 180. To this day, I don't know the course we were supposed to be on.

Our ship was credited with shooting down seven Japanese planes.

Subsequent to my discharge in May of 1945, I attended and graduated from Gettysburg College, and then the University of Pennsylvania School of Veterinary Medicine, all under the GI Bill of Rights.

I graduated from vet school in June of 1953, and set up a small animal veterinary practice with my brother in Camp Hill, Pennsylvania. In 1995 I retired after 40 years practice.

In retirement, along with my wife, we maintain a vineyard not far from Gettysburg. We have three children.

JOHN FULLAM

I was born in 1921 on a farm in Gardenville, Bucks County, Pennsylvania. I attended a one-room country school in Gardenville, then went to Doylestown High School, and graduated in 1938. From there I went to Villanova College (now Villanova University), and graduated in 1942. Upon graduation I was commissioned an ensign in the US Navy. I reported for duty on October 1, 1942 at Cornell University, for basic training, and then was sent to Harvard University for further training in communications. I was then assigned to the *USS Guadalupe* (AO 32) as Communications Officer.

John Fullam

I joined the ship in January 1943 in Adak, in the Aleutian Islands, where she was supporting efforts to contain Japanese forces on Attu, at the end of the Aleutian chain. After that episode concluded (with the withdrawal of the Japanese), the Guadalupe returned briefly to San Pedro, California for overhaul, then spent the balance of 1943 and 1944 in a series of operations throughout the central and western Pacific -- with T.U. 16 in the Gilberts campaign, with Vice Admiral Mitscher's carrier force during the Truk campaign, the Marianas campaign, and various actions in the Palau and Philippine areas, culminating in the climactic Battle of Leyte Gulf in October 1944.

In late December 1944 the Guadalupe sailed from Ulithi as part of Task Force 38 in the first venture into the South China Sea, in support of the invasion of Lingayen Gulf. As the ships were proceeding in close formation through the passage between Luzon and Formosa, another tanker experienced a rudder failure and collided with the Guadalupe, creating a large hole in her bow, but by shifting cargo and making temporary repairs she was able to continue with the carrier force and complete the mission.

In February 1945, the Guadalupe conducted more fueling-at-sea operations in support of the invasions of Iwo Jima and Okinawa.

After returning to California for permanent repairs, the Guadalupe was ordered back to the Okinawa area for the anticipated assault on the Japanese mainland, but shortly after her departure from San Francisco the war ended. The ship was then sent from Okinawa to Korea, in support of (friendly) landings there.

I served aboard the Guadalupe slightly more than three years, principally as Communications Officer, but later as Navigator. During that time I experienced four typhoons and a few tense moments. My service ribbons sport eight combat stars (based on mere proximity to where others were actually fighting).

Upon being discharged from the Navy in April 1946, I entered Harvard Law School, and graduated in 1948. I practiced law in Bristol, Bucks County, Pennsylvania, until I became a Judge of the County Court in February 1960. In 1966, President Lyndon Johnson appointed me to the US District Court in Philadelphia. After a stint as Chief Judge of that court, I assumed Senior status in 1991, but continue to handle a full share of cases.

I married in 1950; my wife was a student at Radcliffe, and we met at a faculty tea while I was in law school. We have four children (two lawyers, an M.B.A. and an artist/educator) and four grandchildren.

FRED GUENTHER

I was born November 20, 1926 in Philadelphia, Pennsylvania. In 1941 the family left the center of the city and moved to Germantown while I was in Jay Cooke Junior HS. I subsequently attended and graduated from Germantown High School Class of June 1944. In July I began pre-veterinary course at the University of Pennsylvania and finished the first semester in September and in October started my second semester. I turned 18 in November and received my draft notice, applied for an educational extension, but was denied. I was drafted January 30, 1945, two weeks before my second semester finals. Penn generously gave me credit for both semesters as I entered military service.

Fred Guenther

I was sent to Indiantown Gap during a period of heavy snows. I had taken typing in high school and was assigned a desk job while my fellow inductees were shoveling snow from the tracks. My desk assignment lasted long enough for me to get one weekend pass home. Basic training was in Camp Blanding, Florida; weather was cold that winter and there was some ice. My fellow trainees were mostly from South Philadelphia or Baltimore, city guys, and on maneuvers they were virtually lost in the woods; if it wasn't concrete they didn't really know what to do. While at Penn I had signed up for the ROTC course. I had acquired basic military knowledge and was familiar with handling/reassembling a rifle. I was assigned as squad leader and thus pulled KP duty or guard duty only once. After basic training we went home on a brief leave. While en route home the news of Germany's surrender gladdened our hearts

After the leave I returned to Ft. Meade for assignment and given the option, European or the Asiatic Theatre, I replied the European for I speak a little German. German quota was full and it was Asiatic for me. We boarded a troop train but were not told our destination. All station signs had been removed; we knew we were headed west and recognized nothing until we reached Chicago. Eventually we arrived at a West Coast military camp somewhere in Oregon, near Corvallis. We trained there for a month. From there we were moved to an embarkation base on San Francisco Bay. While getting ready to board ship we learned the first atomic bomb had been dropped on Japan. Our troopship was three days out from the Golden Gate Bridge when the formal peace was signed with Japan. On that technicality I was awarded the Asiatic-Pacific ribbon. The troops on board were to be part of the invasion force of the Japanese homeland; destination diverted because the war was finished. Our ship was under blackout and did not steer a straight course for the next ten days in case any Japanese submarines were still in a battle mode. Our first landfall was Honolulu bay and we sat for three days with a magnificent view of Diamond Head and then we sailed off, roughly in a Southwesterly direction. We stopped again for a day at some tiny coral atoll, with coconut trees and some shacks. At sea again, the phosphorescent glow of the roiled seas at night was a sight to behold. We were at sea for 30 days before disembarking on the island of Luzon.

Transport was by narrow gauge railway to a tent camp for replacements, isolated in a green canopy away from all habitation. While there I suffered a toothache and dental care was successfully provided using a foot-powered drill rig. Two weeks later we reversed and took the rail back to port and onto another troopship, the SS Sea Bass, destination unknown. While at sea we were hit by a typhoon and I had one of the wildest boat rides I had ever experienced. The bow gyrated up and down in 20-foot swings with some simultaneous sideways swoops. It was on this 36-hour ride that I first tasted coffee. The weather cleared and we unloaded on the island of Okinawa and set up camp on a barren hillside in pup tents with a mess tent nearby. We had settled into an unstructured routine when another typhoon hit. As the tents blew out we were free to seek shelter on our own. Walking was accomplished by leaning into the wind and forging three steps forward and being blown two steps back. My tent mate and I found shelter in the cab of an empty truck. It blew out in a day. Our tents were gone, my stuff was gone, and there was no organization for the next day or so; K rations sustained us. Total time on Okinawa was two weeks and then all camp mates boarded another ship.

We had a short voyage to Inchon harbor in South Korea, then a small group traveled by train to Pusan, Korea and an assignment to a Field Artillary Battalion housed in a former Korean orphanage. This group was assigned the duty of patrolling the local Red Light District to exclude access by our forces. Once again my typing skills afforded me another desk job and I was there for six months through a very cold winter. I later learned that our fellow troop ship mates were housed in tents on the river plain outside of Seoul and they were very cold. The Japanese had been military occupiers of Korea since 1931 and they had impoverished this nation. We were welcomed with open arms. All Koreans were driven to learn English and as a consequence I eventually spent a year in Korea and did not learn more than please and thank you; an educational opportunity wasted. In my free time I explored the community and the hillsides that ringed this coastal city.

After six months, there was a shuffling in the command structures and I traveled by train to the capital city of Seoul. My new assignment was to the Chemical Warfare division of XXIV Corps Headquarters. The Chemical Warfare office, I found, consisted of a major and me, the typing secretary. The duties of this office were to write up the reports of accidents between the military and civilians. My major was regular army and error-proof reports were required; no erasures permitted. My typing skills were not error-proof and as a result many, many discards hit the circular file before the error-proof report emerged. In retrospect I must thank my major, for those six months really enhanced my typing skills and honed my skill at anger management and patience; temper tantrums are not regular army. My quarters were in a three-story former hotel near headquarters. I lived on the third floor with four other clerks assigned to other offices. The mess hall was also centrally located. There were sporadic skirmishes at the 38th parallel, the boundary with North Korea. As a result all personnel carried carbines for show; show only, for we were given no ammunition. Again, my leisure activity was hiking the city and countryside. By the summer of 1946, everyone was counting points; points assigned based on length of service and other factors that did not apply to me. I was hoping for enough points to be discharged and return to Penn for the September semester.

I did not have enough points, so when an opportunity came for a 10-day leave for R&R (Rest and Recuperation) in Japan, I signed on. I took a train back to Pusan; a steamer to Japan and a train north to Nara, an idyllic area of gardens, Buddhist temples; an area untouched by the war. On the train north and on return the tracks went through the outskirts of Hiroshima. I saw the tower-like structure that remains in the center of that city's utter destruction; all that was left after the atom bomb. I feel I owe my life to the fact that the bomb brought an end to the war. Our troopship from Oakland Bay was loaded with infantry destined for the invasion of the Japanese Islands. (An invasion with anticipated major loss of life on both sides of the conflict.) Eventually the point total sufficed and I was on a troopship headed for home. No wandering, no stops and we cheered as we passed once more beneath the Golden Gate Bridge and another train ride cross country to Fort Meade in Maryland in late October '46. My dental health had deteriorated further and it was settled that I had a weekly dental appointment on base until several inlays and bridges were in place. Between appointments I had leave and headed home. This finally ended my army career with the rank of Tech Sergeant; my discharge date is listed as December 16, 1946 and my life resumed.

The spring semester pre-veterinary course at Penn started in February. Before classes I had time to activate the GI bill which paid my tuition for all but my senior classes in the Veterinary School. I also signed on to the 52-20 club. (Actually an unemployment program that paid $20 weekly until employment was gained for a period not longer than 52 weeks.) I went to the Germantown unemployment office faithfully and never once was offered an opportunity for an interview, nor did I seek one. I was living at home for the balance of my education and commuting by train, the Chestnut Hill local from Germantown to 30th Street Station and then a walk to the campus.

I completed the spring semester, and a summer school session followed by the fall '47, spring '48 completion of my pre-veterinary courses to permit acceptance and fall '48 matriculation in the University of Pennsylvania School of Veterinary Medicine to graduate with the class of 1952. Fifty-one men and two women matriculated but only thirty-nine survived to graduate with our class. I signed on with the ROTC for my four years of Veterinary School; one class hour weekly plus six weeks summer camp after our second year. In the fall of '49 a blind date was set up and it clicked. In '50 Ruthe Donecker of Mount Holly, NJ said yes and we married in June of '51, between my junior and senior semesters. I graduated in June of '52 and added Dr. to my name with the Latin designation of VMD. VMD is unique to Penn graduates, other schools offer DVM degrees. I was also a 2nd Lieutenant in the Veterinary Corps Reserves. Interning is not mandatory for veterinary graduates but most seek employment with an established practice to add a practical application to their academic knowledge. Ruthe and I moved to Danville Pennsylvania for my employment with Dr. George Leighow. Our first son, Donald was born in Danville's Geisinger Hospital. Danville is a small rural town so the practice was primarily dairy cow practice, but any farm animal was treated. A few hours daily were devoted to small animal (dog/cat) medicine. A fellow classmate and I had plans to form a partnership in large animal medicine in central Pennsylvania and notice was given to Dr. Leighow; my replacement was interviewed and hired. My intended partner received a draft notice and I was cast adrift and headed home to seek a practice location somewhere in the vicinity of both sets of parents. Three months later, my aunt sent word that the veterinarian in Newtown Pennsylvania had died suddenly and his widow might appreciate help in caring for patients. The veterinarian was Dr. John Hohmiller and after working with his clients for a while, his widow, Peg, agreed to sell me his records and his practice.

We rented in Newtown. Peg handled the phone and made appointments for both large and small animals. We bought an acre and a half of farmland in Newtown Township and started construction of a house with two rooms designated as waiting room and combination exam room/surgery with a kennel room extension of the garage. My buddy from my high school years, best man at our wedding, and graduate architect, designed the entire project. Our contractor was a good friend of my parents. At this time there were far more cows in Newtown Township than there were people. By 1968 the tide had changed, cows had departed and suburban housing greatly increased the pet population. The Newtown Veterinary Hospital plans were assembled with the help of a veterinary architect for the interior and my best man did the exterior design. The hospital was a monthly award winner among nationwide designs submitted.

In 1974, Ruthe and I joined a church travel group to view the 300th anniversary performance of the Passion Play in Oberamergau, Germany. On an extension of that tour we traveled to the Yorkshire Dales of James Herriot, author of "All Creatures Great and Small." I met the esteemed author and his sidekick Tristan. In reality the former is actually Alf Wight and his foil is Brian Sinclair. We visited Brian and his wife Sheila in their home. I had always participated in organized veterinary medicine and had been on the Board of Trustees of the Pennsylvania Veterinary Medical Association since the early '60's. I had also been elected as President and served two terms for the Bucks-Montgomery VMA. During the 1980 annual meeting, I was elected Vice President of the State VMA and subsequently entered the office of President for 1982. Our annual meeting concludes with a renowned speaker and for the 1982 convention, the 100th anniversary of the founding of the PVMA, I invited Brian Sinclair to speak. Brian has a twinkle in his eye and a sense of humor to match. Brian verified the truth of many of the tales but often the actual identity of the protagonists was switched.

I will close with a Herriot-like tale. Jasper was a middle-aged overweight beagle owned by Anna who was past middle age and moved about with difficulty. I usually made house calls to visit Jasper for his minor needs but on occasion I would pick him up and drive him about a mile to my veterinary hospital for his medical care. One day, Charlotte, the receptionist, called me to the front door and there stood Jasper on three legs with one sore paw elevated. Jasper came in and had his paw treated. Anna was called and was relieved for he had gone out and did not return. She was also mystified that Jasper had known the route to the hospital when he needed help (and without an appointment).

GLENN HALL

I was born December 10, 1925 in Windsor, York County, Pennsylvania. I graduated from Red Lion High School in York County, Pennsylvania, in the spring of 1943. In the fall of 1943 I enrolled at Lebanon Valley College in Annville, Pennsylvania.

When I turned 18 in December of 1943, I became eligible for the draft, and entered the Navy in March of 1944. I did my basic training at Sampson, New York. After my basic training I was sent to Bainbridge, Maryland to learn to become a hospital corpsman. My eyesight was so poor they put me on limited or restricted service. My first assignment was night duty, at a hospital. I was assigned to work with a local carpenter, carry his tools around while he did minor repairs

Glenn Hall

in the hospital. One day we happened to be working in the office and I overheard a conversation with a Chief calling names to be transferred out of this base. I asked the Chief if he wouldn't put me on the next out-going list. Two days later, we were in the Chief's office again, and he said to me "I have this thing here you might be interested in." He said. "It's an APA." I said, "What's an APA?" He said, "Attack Personnel Amphibious." So he put me on the list, and the first thing I knew I was shipping out. It was now late summer in 1944 and I was aboard a train headed for the West Coast, Astoria, Oregon to be exact. Our first trip to sea was for our break-in trials, our "Shakedown Cruise." Some of the guys got seasick, but fortunately I was spared the misery. Our first official assignment was to head south along the West Coast to San Francisco to pick up troops and take them to Hawaii.

We were now bound for the Pacific. About this time the war in Europe was coming to a close and many of the troops were being transferred to the Pacific. We got a group of hospital corpsman from the European Theater. They had been in Sicily and D-Day in Europe. They were a tough bunch. I remember one guy named Casey. I'll never forget him, a little short Irishman. One day, during a landing exercise, he was on the beach and it was a mess, apparently everybody was all screwed up. He got on the phone and called back to the ship, and wanted to know who the hell was in charge of this goddamned thing. He didn't know it, but he was talking to our skipper. The Captain said, "Who am I talking to? Who is this?"

And the guy said, "I'm Casey." And he went on and on. Well, it turns out that he was ordered back to the ship to report to the Captain. It ended up that he became the Captain's driver.

Our ship was a troop transport, so our main function was to ferry troops to the battle zone. We were loaded with troops for Okinawa. On our arrival at the place of debarkation, the troops would scramble down a rope ladder into various kinds of landing craft to be taken ashore. This was one of the times that Tokyo Rose said, " We know who you are and where you are going."

On one occasion we hit a typhoon. We were on our way to Okinawa. It was quite an experience. We didn't often travel in convoy, but on this occasion there were large ships in front of us and the waves were so big that when the bow went down in a wave the stern or fantail would rise up, out of water and the screws (propeller) would come completely out of water making a thunderous roar.

We traveled around most of the Pacific ferrying troops. Sometimes we would get back to the States to bring more troops to the far Pacific in preparation for the invasion of Japan. We picked up troops on Saipan or Guam and headed for the invasion of Okinawa. We didn't make the initial landing, but after dispersing our troops we took wounded aboard back to Guam. We remained at Guam until the end of the war. When we were ferrying troops from Okinawa to Guam I became a pharmacists mate. When the war ended, we ferried occupation troops from Okinawa to Japan. We landed our occupation troops at some little fishing village on one of the main islands in southern Japan. Then we got a chance to go ashore ourselves.

After delivering our occupation troops to Japan and a short liberty ashore we received orders to return to the States. On our way to the Panama Canal we experienced some rough seas. After passing through the canal, which was a fascinating experience, we ported in Norfolk, Virginia. The ship was eventually decommissioned there.

Our troop ship was called the *USS Granville*. We were named after a county in North Carolina. However, there was a movie actress, of little fame, by the name of Bonita Granville. We tried to get her to visit our ship, but she said, "No thanks, fellas." Our ship was commissioned at Portland, Oregon in November 1944. She initially carried troops to the central Pacific early in 1945 and then in April and May of 1945 carried troops to Okinawa. After completing that mission she brought casualties back to the US from the western Pacific combat zone, then returned to Okinawa to take occupation troops to Japan. Her final big effort was to bring troops home again from the Pacific in an operation called "Magic Carpet," from October 1945 to January 1946.

I was granted a 30-day leave beginning May 1, 1946. Then all of a sudden, while on leave, I looked at the calendar; it was May 31, I was AWOL (Away With Out Leave). I returned to the Philadelphia Navy Yard anyhow, a day late. A young ensign was going to throw the book at me, but a Chief Carpenters Mate, who was really in charge, said he would take care of the situation, and from there I was discharged.

In the fall of 1946 I returned to Lebanon Valley College under the GI Bill.

After graduating from college in 1949, I again returned home to the people who raised me. My adoptive father was a veteran of World War I, and was in bad health. He operated a small grocery store in a small town in York County. He entered the Veterans Hospital in Lebanon, Pennsylvania, so I took over the grocery store business for a couple of years. I sold that, and went back to college to graduate school at George Washington University for a master's degree.

I did a little teaching, then went to Penn State University for a doctorate. While there I was offered a teaching job at a community college in Florida, near St. Augustine. Then I was offered a graduate assistantship at Penn State and at the same time, I got a Fulbright Grant to teach in the Netherlands. So obviously, I took the Fulbright. I never went back for my doctorate. My wife and I moved to Bucks County in 1965 to take a teaching job at the newly established Bucks County Community College. I was the first teacher hired, and after fourteen years of teaching I became Dean of Academic Affairs. I then returned to the faculty and retired in January 1989.

Since my retirement, I have lived just outside of Newtown, Bucks County, Pennsylvania. I have done a variety of things. I have worked as a census taker, I taught evening classes at the local college, and wrote a history of football for my alma mater, Lebanon Valley College. Then, I had the arduous task of mowing my own lawn, and taking care of the rest of the property.

My wife and I were married in 1953. Gloria has a degree in nursing from Union Memorial Hospital in Baltimore. We have a daughter and two grandchildren.

LOU HOEGSTED

I was born in Chicago, Illinois on September 5, 1915. Most of my early life was spent in Bradley, Illinois.

I graduated from high school in Bradley in June 1933. In early March 1934, I enlisted in the Navy in Indianapolis, Indiana for a four-year term. I served on the Yarnell, a four-stack destroyer, which formed a division with the Tarabell, Upshaw, and Greer. After service in the Pacific, our division was reassigned to the Norfolk area. There I was transferred to the *USS Chandler*, another four-stacker. Over the next several years, we engaged in battle maneuvers up and down the coast. In the same period, we were also in the Pacific, and ventured as far south as the equator.

Lou Hoegsted

When my term of enlistment expired, I went into the Naval Reserve.

In May 1940, reserves were called back into service, and I was assigned to the Great Lakes Naval Training Station for retraining. I remember a chief petty officer telling us we would soon be at war. When the United States entered the war in December 1941, I was transferred with 180 others to San Diego, California, where I was assigned to a gun crew on the *USS Kiltey*, with 12 men under me for training. At the end of our training we were posted to the *SS Meriwether Lewis*, a merchant ship built by the Kaiser Ship Company in Portland, Oregon.

Our shakedown cruise took us to San Francisco, where we took on board a National Guard artillery unit from North Carolina. We also carried ammunition and general Army cargo. We transported them to Brisbane, Australia and then to Noumea, New Caledonia, where we unloaded the ship. The mission was to protect an air base being built up in the mountains, a part of a deployment designed to protect Australia from a Japanese attack.

In 1942 we headed back across the Pacific. With stops in New Zealand to pick up wool and at Iquique, Chile for nitrates, we headed through the Panama Canal into the Caribbean. We learned that there was a German outpost with a view of the canal that was radioing information about the ships passing through to German submarines lurking in the Caribbean. A ship ahead of us was torpedoed as we passed through the Canal. We headed up the coast of Mexico, trying to avoid the submarines, when we encountered one near Little Corn Island, and fired on it. We made it safely to Key West, Florida, where we waited to join a convoy that would take us to Charleston, South Carolina. There we unloaded our nitrates. We were assigned to the *SS Collis B. Huntington*, which was newly commissioned in Wilmington, North Carolina. I was assigned to the gun crew.

Our first stop was Bayonne, New Jersey, where we picked up railway engines, rails, and other equipment for railroads. We were destined for Basra, in Persia, but we never got there. Our convoy changed course, and the ship behind us didn't get the signal and plowed into us. We returned to Bayonne, where I went on leave. I came back to an assignment at the Armed Guard Center in Brooklyn, where I was reassigned to the *SS Exchange*. It carried more guns than we could handle, so we co-opted some army personnel to help out. We made a couple of trips to Europe, carrying 700-800 soldiers on each trip.

Lt. George Perry Corbet recommended me for a commission, so I became an Ensign. Enlisted men who became officers were called "Mustangs."

My next assignment, in June 1944, was to the LSM program at Little Creek, Virginia. We picked up our new vessel, the LSM-215, in Philadelphia, and went down the coast, staying as close to shore as possible. In November or December we were reassigned to the Pacific, passing through the Panama Canal to San Diego. There we made several landings, and at Coronado Beach, San Clemente, as well.

We headed from there across the Pacific, with our first stop at Pearl Harbor. At this point our officers weren't working well together. Our anchor got fouled by a mine cable with mines attached. The propeller was also affected. So we went into dry dock, where we had to wait for a new propeller. We had already been loaded with tanks and armored trucks, and with men of the 5th Marines for the invasion of Iwo Jima. They all had to be unloaded.

We were assigned temporarily to other duties. Finally, we went from there to Guam and then to the Russell Islands and Okinawa. We never did go ashore on Okinawa. Soldiers came aboard and unloaded the equipment. It was a crew of shell-shocked GIs who needed a break from the front.

I remember a fellow named Ralph Behar who had committed some infraction. I told him to put himself on report, and we would convene a captain's mast. Later in the day I asked him if he had done it, and he replied, "No, I decided to give myself another chance." I thought that was pretty funny, so I just forgave him and never said anything.

When the war ended, I returned to Illinois, settled in Aurora and took a job with a lumber company. One day in 1947 or 1948, a man walked in to make a purchase, and I recognized him as Passmore, our cook-striker. Later, working for another lumber company in Champaign, Illinois, I ran into Dick Adams, our Quartermaster. Later, I was transferred in my salvage operation to Massilon, Ohio. There I ran into DeVault, whom I had had to bust down from Cook Third Class to seaman. I was embarrassed!

My son was born in 1948. Both he and his older sister graduated from the University of Georgia. In the Vietnam War he was in the ROTC for about 18 months, stationed in Washington D.C.. For the last 20 years or so he has been in Naples, Florida. For most of that time he worked in the real estate division of Westinghouse Electric. He also served as controller of the First Baptist Church in Naples.

My wife and I came here to Lady Lake, Florida in 1986, shortly after I was operated on for colon cancer. My doctors estimated that I would live another two to five years, but fifteen years later I am still going strong. In 1989 I was employed by the United States Government as a census-taker for the 1990 census. My next job, which I still have, was in a chain grocery store, where at the age of 86 I am still working, part-time, five days a week. Longevity runs in my family. Everyone on both my father's and my mother's side lived well into their 80's or 90's.

I was one of 15 or 16 who attended the second reunion of our LSM crew at Covington, Kentucky in 1990. My job and my wife's health have kept me from more recent gatherings.

PARRY JONES

(as written by his son, Daffydd Jones)

Parry and Lisa Jones

Parry was born on March 31, 1919, to John and Catherine Jones in Wrexham, Wales. When he was a very small child his family moved back to their ancestral village of Llanuwchllyn, located at the end of Lyn Tegid (Bala Lake), before moving to Machynlleth, where Parry spent his formative years. The family had for generations been in the wool business, along with several associated trades. Parry grew up thinking he would join the business and, after attending nearby boarding schools, enrolled for a year in the Llysfasi Agricultural Institute in the fall of 1937, before moving to the Bangor branch of the University of Wales, which specialized in the sciences.

At this time, Hitler was expanding the borders of Germany, and young men were enlisting in the British armed services. Over the course of his first year in Bangor, and with the help and counsel of his friend Hugh Wynn Griffith, among others, Parry made the decision to become a conscientious objector (CO), in spite of being frequently contacted by his local recruiting agent, although both Parry's brothers enlisted. Parry has said he was the only CO in Machynlleth. The British Government recognized CO status, and applicants were required to appear before a tribunal which would produce one of four outcomes, ranging from not believing the applicant to being granted unconditional CO status. He appeared, and stated his case, and was granted unconditional status, based on his beliefs.

During a visit home, an old Quaker friend of his mother told him about the Friends Ambulance Unit (FAU), and she suggested he apply. He did, and was accepted in the fall of 1939. After receiving strenuous training, he arrived in London, probably around January of 1940, and stayed through most of the Blitz, helping to rescue people in the sites of the bombings. He then sailed to India, via Durban, South Africa, arriving in Bombay in February of 1942. He took a train across India, with five other FAU volunteers, to Calcutta. After a month of frustrating work, he hitched a ride on one of the first flights, "over the hump" into Kunming, China, in a DC-3. ("We're pretty sure of our route, but we're still working it out.")

Kunming was the base of operations for the FAU in China, and Parry spent four years participating in and leading truck convoys on the Burma Road, transporting medical relief supplies. The trucks were American 1-ton, outfitted to carry as much as 4 tons. They ran on charcoal, not as steam power, but rather burning one of the gases produced by the combustion of charcoal, which was then injected into the cylinders. They had very little power at all, but the fuel was available. There are many stories, some of them hilarious, some of them horrifying, and some of them both, about driving in any weather on dirt roads or mud roads or worse, over mountain ranges in badly overloaded trucks. Each year the "Northwest Convoy" traveled 2,500 kilometers to the edge of the Gobi Desert and returned with barrels of fuel. Parry went twice, first as a driver, and the next year as a driver and leader of the convoy. Toward the end of the four years in China, he worked with a Catholic Priest, Father Frasinetti, to try to alleviate a famine orchestrated by Chiang Kai-shek's party and, in so doing, upset some local political figure, who decided to bring him in and talk to him. Parry left China hurriedly knowing they were looking for him.

After leaving China at the end of the war, Parry passed through India and arrived back in London before Christmas 1945, to spend the holiday at home with his parents and three siblings, all of whom survived the war. In March of 1946, still with the FAU, he sailed to Bombay to work with Adrian Mayer in Madras on distributing powdered milk to students who were endangered by a famine. Parry was there for about two years, during which time he tried, without success, to get accepted by a Quaker college in America. By chance, he met an American professor, who was instrumental in getting him accepted at Swarthmore College.

As an older student, he was given credit for his life experience, and graduated in three years. While at Swarthmore he was introduced to a younger student, Elise (Lisa) Faulkner, from Massachusetts, but neither of them ever suspected they would later marry. A couple of years later, he visited some friends at the New Hampshire vacation home of Lisa's family, and they started dating after that. They were married on August 15, 1953, in Brookline, Massachusetts. None of Parry's family made it to this country for the wedding. After the wedding, Parry taught at Friends Select School in Philadelphia, while Lisa finished her degree at Swarthmore. They spent two years in Lahore, Pakistan, working on family planning, before returning to the States. In the fall of 1958, Parry began teaching history at George School, in Bucks County, Pennsylvania. During 1964 and 1965, he was enrolled in graduate studies at the University of Pennsylvania, and then taught history at Princeton Day School from 1966 until his retirement in 1979. Parry was vocal throughout his life about his support for the Civil Rights movement, joining Martin Luther King for the last day of his march from Selma to Montgomery, Alabama. He was also opposed to the Vietnam War, which he demonstrated in Washington D.C..

Parry and Lisa have three boys: Owen, Daffydd and Gwyn, and four grandchildren.

Compiler's Note: Parry died in 2004.

BOB KENDERDINE

Bob Kenderdine

On April 16, 1926 I was born in Trenton, New J, but have lived in Newtown all my life. I graduated from high school in Newtown in 1943.

In August 1944, I went to the chairman of the Draft Board, Aubrey Merrick, and told him I was ready to be drafted. He called my father, to whom I hadn't yet spoken about my plan, and my father said the decision was mine, if that is what I wanted to do. Charlie Sutton, a friend, joined me in signing up. I went down to Philadelphia, took the physical, and was assigned to New Cumberland Gap. After a short period there, I was assigned to Camp Crawford, North Carolina, for infantry basic training. Most of my colleagues stayed in the infantry, and ended up in the Battle of the Bulge. But in October, I was assigned to an artillery unit at Fort Bliss, Texas. Shortly after getting there, I came down with scarlet fever and spent three weeks in the hospital. Following a five-day leave at home, I was assigned to Seattle, Washington. From there we were shipped to Honolulu. It took us two weeks--of high seas, miserable weather, and seasickness--to complete a journey that usually took four or five days.

Except for a brief excursion to another Pacific Island, where we were held in reserve and never shot at, I spent the rest of the war in Pearl Harbor, and got back home in August of 1946.

When the Korean War broke out, I had no desire to serve as a private, so I joined the Reserves, where I achieved the rank of Master Sergeant. I spent the war at Fort Benning, Georgia, and came back to Newtown when the war ended.

My family migrated to the United States in about 1736, settled in the Horsham area, and then moved to Lumberville. My great great grandfather, Thaddeus Kenderdine, named for the poet and abolitionist Thaddeus Stephens, moved to Newtown in 1872. He started a feed business, and was instrumental in getting the railroad to Newtown from Philadelphia, to carry his products to the city. The original station was near the present site of the Whistle Stop Restaurant, now the Sports Bar. He and his brother took up farming where the 7-11 is now. My great uncle's son took over the business, and lost it during the depression of the 1930s. Shortly thereafter, my father and grandfather reopened it, selling coal for many years from a site with its own siding just north of the railroad. I took over the business, and ran it for about 40 years. I converted to oil, and finally sold it and retired in 1991.

WALTER KONICKY

I was born on September 3, 1919 in Johnstown, Pennsylvania. I was one of six children, and my mother died at a very early age. I spent a lot of time in an orphanage with a brother and sister. Twice I was farmed out to do farm labor like a slave. I suffered all kinds of indignation and degradation. I felt like my prisoner of war experience was an extended and greatly magnified continuation of my childhood.

Walter Konicky

After graduating from high school in Johnstown, Pennsylvania, I worked in the steel mill there for several months, and then got laid off. When I couldn't find another job, I thought "the hell with it," and decided to join the army.

They sent me to Fort Slocum, New York, and then they put me on a ship, the *USS Grant*, and sent me directly to the Philippines. It took 45 days aboard ship to go from New York to the Philippines. We landed in Manila on the island of Luzon. I can't remember the date, but it was before Pearl Harbor. There is where I did my basic training.

Germany invaded Poland, and we were on our way to the Philippine Islands. I guess the war started for us when the Japanese bombed Pearl Harbor, and then they bombed Manila the next day.

We had been fighting for only a couple of months before we were captured. I developed malaria, and got a real high fever of 105° Fahrenheit, and was sent back to the field hospital. I was in the hospital when they bombed it. It seemed like everybody came out with their hands up, and surrendered the entire island, best that I can recollect.

That was the beginning of the "Bataan Death March." Just that quick. We marched about 60 kilometers for five days and five nights of steady marching. No food at all. That was rough. We marched to Camp O'Donnell. You probably have heard stories of Camp O'Donnell. That was real bad. From there we went to Cabanatuan, where I spent one day in Bilabed prison. We were mixed in with Philippine prisoners who were in shackles with whom we spent the night. From there they put us on a ship and shipped us to Japan, on work details, lasting 42 months, almost four years.

They were pulling out groups of 400 or 500 people who were in prison camp and sending them to Japan on work details. Then we went through a typhoon while in the hold of a ship; everybody was sick. What a mess! When we got off the ship in Japan, people were staring and sneering at us. That is when they marched us into Osaka to the prison camp where we were interned. The death march once more. In prison camp, we were fed a starvation diet. We had no medicine or help from doctors.

After the death march, I spent my entire time as a POW in Japan, a total of 42 months.

I spent a lot of my later military service at Fort Dix, New Jersey and in my retirement moved to Morrisville, Pennsylvania where I still reside.

My wife and I have three children, two boys and a girl.

Compiler's Note:

The following is a mixture of information from the Internet and the original interview:

'Just after the bombing of Pearl Harbor, the Philippine Islands were invaded by the Japanese. We were defending the island for three months before we surrendered, and became prisoners of war; consequently we were already in a weakened condition, with limited food and low on ammunition. Just before my capture, and the start of the "Death March", I was in a hospital with malaria and a high fever of 105° Fahrenheit. The day of the Death March, April 10, 1942, the Japanese bombed the hospital I was in, and from there I was subject to the five-day march with no food or water, and considered a POW for 42 months.'

'Prisoners of war were beaten randomly and denied food and water for days. Those who fell behind were executed through various means: shot, beheaded or bayoneted. The commonly used Japanese "sun treatment" forced a captive to sit in the humid April sun without water or even the shade of his helmet.

'About 10,000 perished, some escaped while approximately 40,000 reached camp.'

Compiler's Note:

In addition to the author's interview with Mr. Konicky, we wish to include some excerpts from his response to questions asked by the office of the Veterans Administration (Out-patient Clinic) in Philadelphia, a letter addressed to his home in Pennsylvania in 1986, requesting his experiences during internment.

'Beatings and torture were witnessed numerous times. One captive was forced to kneel on the rung of a ladder, sit back on his heels, and then was clubbed across the thighs. This individual died in camp, was placed in the fetal position in a barrel-like container, and was taken out of camp. Another captive was backed against a wall with a water hose jammed in his mouth and the water pressure on.

Each time he tried to resist, the guard would beat him. One captive in the Philippines was tied to a fence post naked in the hot burning sun all day. The Japanese guards would poke and spit on him when passing by. In the Philippines we witnessed the execution of several captives. They dug their own graves; then with hands tied behind their backs and kneeling, they faced a Japanese firing squad.

We were intimidated daily. For bobbing and swaying in rank one day, a guard gave me a left hook to the jaw, and a kick in the shins. On another occasion, while I was bending down using a shovel, a guard came up behind me, and when I stood up to see what he wanted, he accused me of trying to attack him. From this point on, they had me identified as a trouble-maker. They tried to make us do impossible tasks, like pushing loaded box cars. When we were too weak to do so, they reported us to camp for resisting. They favored mass punishment, and used this form of intimidation quite often.

Six captives in the group I worked with, myself included, received floggings with a water soaked hawser across the buttocks, and then were immersed for a specified period in a tank of ice water up to our necks. On another occasion, I had a boil inside my groin, and when I received the first blow, I dropped to my knees. A guard made me stand to the side, and when he finished with the rest of them, I received some 30 lashes (head and face) with a wide military belt. This beating caused my eyes to nearly close, due to excessive swelling, and put large blisters on my ears. I had the appearance of Mongolism for a long time, with blurred vision and ringing in my ears. This did not excuse me from work. The Japanese workers at the mill would point at me and snicker.

We gave the guards names according to their temperament, like "Air Raid", "Cyclone", "Slinky", "Legal Twenty", and "Donald Duck". Although we treated all guards with a jaundiced eye, we were constantly on edge and apprehensive whenever "Air Raid" or "Cyclone" were on duty. Air Raid and Cyclone did all the beatings. And in all the beatings and torture the Japanese commander was absent.

In my judgment, the entire forty months of captivity was a form of solitary confinement, with boring dialogue between somber individuals and nerves at the breaking point, forever on edge due to persistent harassment. In addition, repeated cycles of 13 days continuous labor plus one day in camp doing strenuous calisthenics coupled with constant intimidation, resulted in self-imposed isolation to one's cubicle. Although I did not experience solitary confinement in the true sense, it was experienced by the fact that we were completely shut off from the outside world for the entire three and a half years of captivity. We lost all track of time and didn't know Monday from Friday.

While in captivity, I received no news from home. I was allowed to send one post card home which had been censored with only two words remaining, "doing fine".'

When asked the question, "what was your worst experience?" Walter's reply was, "It is impossible to choose one experience as being the worst. From the day of capture until the day of repatriation, it was a living hell. No one in camp was expected to live through the winter."

Sleeping arrangements: we were packed in like sardines, and slept in straw-padded

Memorial Day Parade, May 29, 2005. Norm Moorehead, Bill Craighead, Walter Konicky and Richard Grasko (Vietnam).

cubicles. Due to lice and flea infestation, the straw padding was removed, and we slept on boards with wide cracks and only one thin blanket.

I worked in excessive heat in the hold of a ship unloading ore and pig iron. I also cleaned debris next to open hearths, and was overcome by gas and passed out. I also loaded hot slag on box cars.

The water was not potable. It had to be boiled, and rationed as green tea. We were given a tea cup of bland rice gruel in the morning. Raw rice was measured, cooked, and then divided equally among all the captives; the serving was one tea cup or less. Those who were sick and unable to work were put on half rations. On occasion, a spoonful of salty bean mash was given. Fish with maggots and a strong smell of ammonia was offered twice, and had to be rejected. Bread in the form of a weevil-infested bun was given no more than six times during our entire captivity.

Pangs of hunger do strange things. We would raid incinerators near the mill for possible discarded bits of rice or fish, taking a chance to suffer beatings in the event we would be caught. In the Philippines, the Japanese would club a dog to death, and take only that portion near the back bone, we would take the rest. In Japan, we would gather tangerine peels along the road on the way to work.

Diseases: I would experience malaria like clockwork daily, with violent chills followed by fever as high as 105° Fahrenheit. Dysentery was prevalent with death as a result, with ever increasing numbers daily. We lived with the fear of exposure to all sorts of affliction. Elephantiasis was experienced, with testicles swollen as large as footballs. Infestation with body lice was due to limited bathing, vitamin deficiency, and burning pain due to pellagra and beriberi. Captives began to suffer broken bones with the slightest exertion.

We were exposed to many diseases, as rats ran across our bodies at night. We had to dig shallow common graves and bury naked bodies so decomposed that the skin would separate from the flesh. Wild dogs would uncover the graves at night.

JIM KURTZ

I was born on September 18, 1921 in the small town of Hillside, New Jersey, between Newark and Elizabeth. I was the fifth of six children. My father immigrated to the United States in 1906 from Bavaria, now Germany. My mother was from Hungary.

I graduated in 1940 from Summerville High School in Summerville, New Jersey.

I grew up on a 160-acre farm, 3 miles north of Princeton, New Jersey.

I enlisted in the Marines. After waiting several months, I was finally notified in June, 1942 to report for active duty. We went from Newark, New Jersey to Paris Island, South Carolina, for eight weeks boot camp training. At the completion of boot camp, I was sent to communications school in Quantico, Virginia for four weeks instruc-

Jim Kurtz

tion on the use of communication equipment, such as radios and telephones, as well as infantry training. From late August to early October 1942, I was sent to Camp Lejeune, North Carolina, to learn how to string communication lines under simulated combat conditions.

After completing this training, four of us volunteered for immediate overseas duty. We left the States on December 4, 1942, aboard the *Day Star*, a freighter converted to a troop ship, and arrived in Pago Pago, American Samoa, 15 days later. We remained there for a week or so, and were then assigned to the 8th Defense Battalion, and relocated to an island guarding the Samoas. A few months later, as military activities moved northward, we relocated several hundred miles north to Wallis Island, part of the French Samoas, to set up defenses while the island was used by our fighter planes to guard against attack by the Japanese.

In mid-November, 1943 we were given four days to prepare to board an LST (Landing Ship Tank) for a three-day trip to Tarawa in the Gilbert Islands. Our mission was to give technical support, in the form of emergency communications and defense. Later we were sent to a nearby island called Abemama, about 100 miles from Tarawa. Here the 8th Defense Battalion again "set up shop" with its anti-aircraft weapons, searchlight units and machine-gun defenses, all linked to headquarters by field telephone lines. Large runways were constructed on this island, using crushed coral for their surfaces. Our bombers flew many missions attacking enemy bases further north. Fighter planes were also stationed here to ward off enemy planes and protect our bombers, especially as they limped home, badly damaged, with dead and wounded aboard, making them an easy target for Japanese fighter planes.

It was at this time that radar, in its early technical stages, was introduced. I was fortunate to be selected to be a technician, plotting friendly and enemy flights heading toward our base of operations. While on these islands, many of us contracted diseases such as: malaria, Dengue fever, and MuMu or elephantiasis (a swelling of the joints). Those disabled were rotated back to the States. After many months duty at Abcmama, and a going-away party, we boarded the *King George*, a British freighter, for the seven-day trip to Pearl Harbor. After spending three days in the Naval Hospital at Pearl Harbor, we boarded the *USS Chandler*, an aircraft tender, for the seven-day trip to San Francisco. We were going home after two long years. We did manage to get several days liberty in "Frisco" before heading to the Naval Hospital in San Diego. After a thorough physical examination into the rarity of our diseases, we were granted a 30-day leave and headed for home.

My homecoming was a great experience. However, mid-way through my 30-day leave, I wound up in the Brooklyn Naval Hospital. After a four or five week stay, I was re-assigned to the Marine Corps Signal Supply Depot in Philadelphia, on limited duty, for approximately seven months. It was here that I met my future wife, Regina, who was working as a civilian for the Corps. We were married in April 1945, and five or six days later I was immediately transferred to the West Coast midway between San Diego and Los Angeles, California, where I was to be reassigned to a unit that would be part of a force invading Japan. Fortunately, the war ended, and I was discharged in September of 1945.

I immediately enrolled in Temple University, under the GI Bill, to pursue a business degree. Our daughter was born in 1946, and a son in 1951. We built our first home in 1950-1951, and I simultaneously started on my business career. For 12 years I was employed by a chemical company with responsibility for five or six small chemical companies. I then took on a position with another chemical company and ended up as vice president with responsibility for plants in the US, Canada, and Europe. I flew on the Concorde many times back and forth to Europe; it was quite an experience. I retired in 1986, and then kept busy as a part-time managing consultant for another ten years.

In our retirement, my wife and I feel very fortunate to be able to travel abroad; in Europe, China, the Caribbean, and Canada, as well as all 50 states.

We have been most fortunate to enjoy a wonderful family, consisting of two children, and their spouses, two grandchildren, and four great grandchildren.

We presently live in a retirement community in the Newtown area, and are in good health, and are gardeners, swimmers, hikers and volunteer workers. We enjoy our winters in Florida.

During the past six years, I have written an unpublished manuscript, titled *"Twentieth Century Odyssey - Just Passing Through"*, an autobiography.

VINCE LEEDOM

I was born on December 3, 1921 in Dolington, Pennsylvania. At the time my parents lived on a farm on Lindenhurst Road.

I went to school in a one-room schoolhouse not far from our farm, about a half a mile away. It is still there, although the surrounding area is quite built up. From there I went to Woodside for the 10th grade. It is now part of the Pennsbury system. At that time they didn't have junior and senior year, so I had to come to the Chancellor Street School in Newtown, and graduated in 1939.

After graduation from high school, I worked for Delaval Steam Turbine in Trenton, New Jersey, until I was drafted in 1944. On May 4,

Vince Leedom

1944, I was able to select the Navy, and did my boot training at Camp Perry, Virginia, just outside of Williamsburg.

After boot camp, I returned home on leave, and came back to the out-going unit and the Navy sent me to basic engineering school in Gulfport, Mississippi for eight weeks. After I graduated from school, they sent me to steam-turbine school at Con Edison in New York City. During that time, I was stationed at Pier 92 in New York City. From there I went to Norfolk, Virginia, with a group of 275 men, and trained aboard three or four destroyers.

After the completion of our training aboard the destroyers, we were sent to Wells Fargo in Boston, Massachusetts. I was part of the crew that commissioned the *USS Sutherland,* DD 743, on Christmas Eve, 1944.

The day before, the Navy had commissioned a sister ship, the destroyer, *USS Fort Knox.* They were both built in Bath, Maine. We went on our shakedown cruise to Bermuda in February 1945. We came back, and they decided they wanted to make it a radar picket ship. So they cut the center out, reinforced it with heavier material, then took the front torpedo tubes off, and put radar equipment on it that stood pretty high.

On April 24, 1945 we rendezvoused with TU 23.16.1 off the New Jersey coast, and then headed for the Pacific, arriving at Pearl Harbor May 15, 1945, Ulithi May 28, and in June to Leyte. On July 1, 1945 she joined TF 38, the fast carrier task force, for the fleet's final raids of the Japanese home islands. From July 10, 1945 until the end of the war, she screened the carriers as their planes flew against military and industrial targets on the Tokyo Plain, in other parts of Honshu, on Hokkaido, and in the Inland Sea. Twice detached for night shore bombardment missions with TU 34.8.1, she fired on the Hamamatsu area, southern Honshu, on the night of July 29th and 30th, and on Kamaishi, northern Honshu, August 9th and 10th, 1945.

Strikes on the Tokyo Plain scheduled for 15 August were cancelled as hostilities ceased, but the ships continued to cruise off the Japanese coast. On the 27th, *Sutherland* anchored at Sagami Wan; and on the 28th, she moved up to Tokyo. On the 30th, she covered the landing occupation troops at Huttu Saki and Yokosuka. A week later, she completed a mail run to the Ryukyus; then joined TG 35.1 for further occupation duty.

The *Sutherland* remained active with the US Navy through 1974. From the time of her commissioning in 1944, she earned one battle star in WW II, eight during the Korean conflict and ten during the tours off Vietnam. She was decommissioned in 1981.

At the end of the war, I was sent home for immediate discharge.

Shortly after I returned home I went back to work for Delaval, in Trenton, New Jersey. I was only there about a week when they went on strike. I then took a job with a friend down on US 1, and from that time I went into the automobile business. I started as a lube boy, and worked my way up as an auto mechanic. When I left I was a parts manager, so I retired after 30 years in the automobile business. Then I went to work for my niece and nephew, which was Leedom's Welding here in Newtown, until I retired.

I was married on June 18, 1942, 63 years ago, and went into the service. We have two daughters and three grandchildren.

We now live in retirement, in the Pickering Manor Apartments, here in Newtown. We enjoy it very much, no grass to cut, no snow to shovel. It's independent living, so you can do what you want.

RAY MANAHAN

I was born in New York City on January 13, 1919. I graduated from McBurney Prep in New York City, and went to Geneva College for my BA degree. Then I went to the University of Pittsburgh for my dental degree (DMD). In January 1945, I was in the specialized Army Program. I did oral surgery as a graduate student at New York University. After graduation, I went into the US Public Health Service, and was commissioned a Lt. j.g. After my internship at a marine hospital in New York City, I went on active duty as a dental officer, and was assigned to the *USS General Meigs*, APA 116, a troop transport in Norfolk, Virginia.

Ray Manahan

It was commissioned on June 3, 1944 in Bayonne, New Jersey. It was owned by the Navy, but operated by the Coast Guard. It had a speed of 25 knots, and was capable of carrying 5,100 troops. It was decommissioned on March 4, 1946 in San Francisco, California.

My first trip was from Naples, Italy to Rio de Janeiro, delivering troops. Rio de Janeiro has one of the most beautiful seaports in the world. The ship was blacked out on this trip because problems with German submarines were still on.

My main duty aboard ship was to serve as dental officer, but I was sometimes given special assignments. On this one occasion, my duty assignment was to take three truckloads of 75 GI's to the Pompeii ruins in Naples, Italy. At the gate, I found out there was an admission charge, which I paid.

One time a GI came aboard with a brain tumor. He died, and was placed in refrigeration. The role and pitch of the ship caused the body to be mixed up with the refrigerated meat. They had to find the smallest guy they could find, to ride the dumb waiter to get the body. (Then nobody knew the difference between the live body and the deceased.)

Another time there was a deck officer, a typical salty kind of guy with twenty years service, and a fondness for alcohol. We were in Karachi, pulling out at midnight, with bow lines already cast. He fell into the sea, and they finally got him aboard, still holding on to his bottle.

We carried troops to Tacloban in the Philippines, Nagoya in Japan, Karachi in India, Port Said in Egypt, and the Suez Canal.

When the war was over they decommissioned my ship in San Francisco. I was then assigned to the US Marine Hospital in Pittsburgh, Pennsylvania. I served in Puerto Rico at the Coast Guard Base, the US Coast Guard Academy in New London, Connecticut, then the US Coast Guard Training Station in Groton CT, and the USA Marine Hospital in New York City.

After terminal leave from the Coast Guard, I enlisted in the US Army to serve in the Korean War. I was assigned to the Dental Corps at Ft. Monmouth, New Jersey, with the rank of captain.

Ray Manahan

I spent five years with the Public Health Service. We were commissioned and were militarized by President Roosevelt, and attached to the Army Engineers-- dentists and physicians mostly went to the Coast Guard. I served in the military, both the Army and Coast Guard, for more than nine years.

My next Army assignment was to Camp Atterbery, Indiana. I received a commendation from the Camp General.

I came to Newtown in 1953 to set up a dental practice, and was active until 1995. During that time I performed dental surgery at Abington Hospital and later at the Philadelphia State Hospital. I served as chief of dental services at Pennhurst State School and Hospital. I continued private practice until 1993.

I married Mary Ellen McGary in 1945, just before shipping out overseas. We have four children: Ray, Marcy, Debra, and Betsy, and nine grandchildren.

My retirement includes traveling, theatre, concerts, and enjoying my grandchildren. I now live at the Friends Home in Newtown.

Ray Manahan

STAN MATTHEWS

Stan Matthews

I was born on November 21, 1926 on Court Street next to the Court Inn, in Newtown, Pennsylvania. I attended the Chancellor Street School in Newtown until the end of my junior year, at which time I enlisted in the Navy. I did my boot camp training at Bainbridge, Maryland for 16 weeks, and at the completion of my boot camp, I stayed there and went to gunnery school for another 16 weeks. My time in the Navy was from September 23, 1944 to October 28, 1947.

I was then sent to Pier 92 in New York, and boarded the destroyer Ordronaux DD 617, on May 5, 1945. After six or seven weeks delay for alterations, we headed for the Pacific through the Panama Canal, arriving at Pearl Harbor on July 24, 1945. From there we went to Wake Island where we had a slight confrontation with the Japanese still occupying it on August 1, 1945, since the US chose to by-pass it.

The Ordronaux was built by the Bethlehem Steel Company, at Fore River, Massachusetts. She was commissioned on February 13, 1943. Her first encounter with the enemy was on July 26, 1943 at Bizert, when she was attacked by German planes, and managed to down three of them. She was in the invasion of Sicily on July 9, 1943. For nearly a year, she was assigned escort duty of convoys across the Atlantic and through the Mediterranean. On April 7, 1944 she assisted in the capture of 28 crewmen after sinking a German submarine. On May 12, 1944, while in the Mediterranean, she supported the US 5th Army advancing on Rome and the beachhead at Anzio. On August 9, 1944, she supported the invasion of Southern France. She returned to convoy duty, and in May 1945 returned to New York for alteration; she then headed for the Pacific through the Panama Canal, arriving at Pearl Harbor on July 24, 1945, and then on to Wake Island. The Ordronaux arrived at Okinawa several days after Japan surrendered. After the surrender, she took part in two occupation landings at Wakayama and Nagoya. She earned three battle stars during WW II.

I boarded the Ordronaux in New York on May 5, 1945, and stayed aboard until she was decommissioned in January of 1947. My only confrontation with the enemy was a brief skirmish at Wake Island, when on August 1, 1945 we shelled the island briefly, and met some accurate counter-fire. I am honored to have served aboard her, for she did her share during the WW II.

Almost 60 years after the war ended, in 2004, Pennsylvania adopted House Bill 186, which passed the State Legislature and was signed by the Governor, authorizing local school boards to grant diplomas to those veterans who did not graduate due to entrance into the military service, provided they had an honorable discharge. They called this event, "Operation Recognition."

I am proud to say that I am a recipient of such a diploma, and am now, officially, a member of the class of 1945, Newtown High School, Newtown, Pennsylvania.

After the war, I worked as a carpenter, and then for 29 years worked for Holland Enterprises here in Bucks County.

I am now retired and enjoy reading, playing pinochle, and spending time with my family, especially my grandchildren.

I married Helen Yates on February 25, 1949. We have two children, both boys, four grandchildren, and two great-grandchildren.

BOB OLSON

I was born in Boston, Massachusetts in June 1924. I lived all my life in Somerville, Massachusetts, a suburb of Boston. When Pearl Harbor was bombed on December 7, 1941, I was a senior in high school. So it was a pretty well drawn conclusion that when I graduated from high school, I would enlist or be drafted into one of the services. When the aircraft carrier, the USS Lexington was sunk in July or August of 1942, the Navy put on a

Hope and Bob Olson

large recruiting campaign in the Boston area, called the "Lexington Volunteers." That was apropos to the Boston area because of the Revolutionary War in Lexington, Massachusetts. This drew me and several of my friends to stop in at the recruiting office and see what it was all about. The Navy recruiters put on a good show, and before we left we signed up as new recruits. When I came home and told my parents, they were surprised. They thought I should have come home and talked it over with them first.

In September of 1942, I was inducted into the Navy and sent to the Great Lakes Naval Training Center in October of 1942 for basic training. After completing boot camp I was sent to a radio school in New York City. That is where I learned to use Morse Code to receive and send messages.

Being in the Navy, radio school, and 18 years old in New York City was exciting. I spent my first New Year's Day away from home in the big city and Times Square.

After radio school, I was assigned to Quonset Point, Rhode Island, which was a Naval Air Station. My first job was to check out the radios in the airplanes. Since I didn't know about the location of radios in airplanes, they reassigned me to the base radio station. During my time at Quonset Point I was in the radio room, learning radio operations. We were responsible for keeping radio contact with all the patrol planes that were running up and down the East Coast, the PBYs and PBMs. We maintained communication with those folks because there was a tremendous amount of activity on the East Coast during 1942 and 1943 with the

German U-boats. That was a very hectic period of time. In command of the air wing at Quonset Point was Admiral Durgan, and he maintained that the escort carrier could be a fighting ship. The old CVE, the escort carrier, was used primarily for escorting other ships. They finally gave him a command and a staff, and I was privileged to have been selected to join his staff. Along with several others, we became radio operators and went aboard the CVE *USS Tulagi.*

We left Quonset Point and headed across the Atlantic for the Mediterranean. The trip through the Mediterranean was rather interesting, but all of a sudden it brought to my attention, for the first time, the realities of war. We went to Alexandria in Egypt, and to Malta, which had been pretty beat up in Rommel's effort to retreat. We saw the toe of Italy and Naples, where we could see the Isle of Capri.

From Naples we then joined some British Forces for the invasion of southern France. This took place just after the Normandy beachhead was established, in June of 1944.

After the invasion of southern France in July of 1944, our carrier, the *USS Tulagi*, received orders to report back to the East Coast. The crew was given leave, and then reassigned to San Diego. It was a long train trip across country. At San Diego we were assigned to another escort carrier, the *USS Makin.*

We left the States and headed for Hawaii, the Admiralties, New Guinea, small atolls, and then the Philippines, before supporting the invasion of Iwo Jima and finally Okinawa. During one attack, our ship managed to shoot down two kamikazes, but two got through our defense. One went off the side of the ship and took the radio antennas with him. The other went through the flight deck on the forward part of the ship into the officer's quarters, where several pilots were killed. At Okinawa, our ship received a Presidential Citation for this action during the kamikaze attack.

At the war's end, we were in the proximity of Japan, and were one of the first ship's crew to go ashore in a small fishing village on the mainland of Japan. They strapped side arms on us, but they took the clips out of our firearms. We walked up and down the streets waving and smiling. Our job was to be friendly, even though we couldn't speak the language. On our return to the ship, another crew did the same thing. We did get to Tokyo and things were a little more relaxed there.

It is amazing to be so far from home and accidentally run into someone you know, completely out of the blue, so to speak. When we pulled into Malta and got off the ship at the dock, I'm standing there waiting for my buddies. At the dock was another ship with sailors waiting to go ashore. There was a friend from my own neighborhood. We went to school together, worked together, and even went to the same church. Then on another occasion, there was a guy I went to school with on another ship in the harbor. We managed to get together for a short time.

When the war was over, it became a matter of when and how to get out. There was a point system. A point for every month in the service and another point for every month overseas. If they added up to a certain number, you then became eligible for discharge. I was fortunate enough to have enough points, and given the option to return home to the States. I was put on a cruiser to return to the States. Once again, while on deck I met a schoolmate from my hometown.

We landed at Long Beach, California. From there we took a train back East. It was packed full of service people, messy, and dirty. It was much worse than my trip across country to the West Coast to pick up my ship on the way to the Pacific.

We finally arrived in South Boston, on December 23,1945. I immediately called my parents. What a blessing, I was home for Christmas. My parents didn't know where I was or when I was expected home. I called them on the phone, and told them where I was, and that I would take a taxi home. All of a sudden I realized I might not have enough money to pay the taxi driver. When I asked the taxi driver how much it would be, he must have heard some of my telephone conversation, and said, "Hop in, it's on me."

I got home Christmas Eve, and then after New Year's Day reported to the discharge center in Boston, where I was officially discharged in February 1946.

In high school I was a soda jerk, and became interested in possibly becoming a pharmacist. On my return, the pharmacist encouraged me to go to pharmacy school. At first I did a lot of odd jobs, including working in the Bursar's Office for the Massachusetts Institute of Technology. I worked very hard; I would work all day and attend night school at Bentley College of Accounting. I also went to Boston College and took business and accounting. While still at MIT I ran into people from IBM, who were modernizing their accounting equipment. The next thing I knew they offered me a job. I started there in 1952, and retired after 35 years of service. I worked for IBM, first in Boston, then to Worcester, Massachusetts; New York City; White Plains; Philadelphia; Trenton, New Jersey; and Valley Forge, Pennsylvania.

I might not have received a full college education, if it hadn't been for the GI Bill of Rights.

My wife Hope was originally from Maine. We met at a church social in Somerville, a suburb of Boston, and were married in 1947. We have three children, all girls, eight grandchildren and one great grandchild.

HOWARD SMITH

I was born in Philadelphia, and lived there through high school. Then my parents moved to a farm near Morrisville, Pennsylvania, some of which became a part of Levittown. My mother, a Jew born in Jerusalem and now in her nineties, and one brother still live there. Our other brother was a paratrooper in the 101st Airborne Division. He died in Europe. My father was an FBI agent for 30 years, working out of New York City. He was killed in the line of duty at age 55.

I enlisted in the Navy in November 1942. After six weeks of boot training, I had three weeks of gunnery training and three weeks of training in underwater demolition. I crossed the Atlantic on a destroyer that was part of the escort of a convoy to England. We supported the invasion of Normandy and went on

Howard Smith

to Italy, where we went ashore. Enemy shore batteries shelled us, destroying one gun turret. We took the destroyer back to the Brooklyn Navy Yard, and I was reassigned to the newly commissioned *USS Johnson*. Except for five weeks on an aircraft carrier, all of my service was on destroyers.

Our ship was redeployed to the Pacific area, where we preceded the landing force, using high explosives to clear the way. It was usually underwater demolition, for which I had had training as a scuba diver, but we blew up any enemy installations we could reach.

Our ship, carrying about 200 men, was sunk in the Battle of the Philippine Sea. Nearby was a Class A aircraft carrier, one of the small ones. It was also hit, and there were about 1,100 men in the water with us. One destroyer near us was sunk, and another one arrived. We were being fired on by Japanese cruisers and battleships, for which we were no match. In fact, one of their vessels was the battleship Yamamoto, which had the biggest guns ever placed on a battleship. They destroyed our bridge, and most of our gun mounts, reducing our operable guns to two. I can't tell you how I managed to survive, because I was unconscious. I learned later that I was moved to a second destroyer, that was also sunk.

I remained unconscious for 38 days, and didn't "come to" until I got back to Pearl Harbor. I was shipped back to the New York Naval Hospital, where I underwent a total of eleven operations, to rebuild my face. I have only four of my own teeth. When my mother first visited me there, she didn't recognize me. I was finally discharged from the service at the Philadelphia Naval Hospital. But I still wake up at night sometimes and jump out of bed, because I hear the big guns going off.

When I returned home to Bucks County, I found the winter weather painful, so I moved to Anaheim, California. I took advantage of the GI Bill of Rights to attend California State University at Fullerton, and bought a house there. I worked for an automobile dealer, and moved up to the job of manager of the dealership.

I have two boys and a girl. My wife and I are divorced.

I retired in 1984 and settled in Brookfield, Florida, on the gulf coast about 40 miles north of Clearwater. I am now in real estate, and remain active. It keeps me from going nuts.

Complier's Note:
Howard died in 2004.

JIM SMITH

(Jim Smith attained the rank of major general in 1980,
having started as a private in 1942.)

Jim Smith

I was born on September 5, 1923, one of three children, two boys and a girl. My brother, two years my junior, now owns and operates a health club in Tampa, Florida. My father was a career Army man, retiring in 1948 as a major. He had enlisted in the Army in 1915, joining the 6th Cavalry, where he rose to the rank of Regimental Sergeant Major, having served on the Mexican border and then in World War I, when he served in France. After the war his regiment spent the inter-war years in Fort Oglethorpe, Georgia. In 1942, he was the most senior noncommissioned officer in the Army. Later that year he was reassigned to Camp Blanding, Florida, to stage for service in Europe. At the end of the war he was Commander of the Reception and Separation Center at Fort McPherson, Georgia.

I enlisted in the army, choosing the cavalry, at Chattanooga, Tennessee on June 29, 1942. It turned out that there was a 90-day backlog of soldiers awaiting cavalry training, so I appealed to a review board, which decided to send me, directly, without basic training, to the 16th Cavalry. Their reason for doing so was the fact that my father had been a regular army cavalry officer. So they sent me directly to Officers Candidate School, at Fort Riley, Kansas, from which I emerged 90 days later, on January 14, 1943, as a shave-tail, or Second Lieutenant.

After service in the 29th Cavalry Regiment, I got my first combat assignment, as a second lieutenant, to the 6th Cavalry Regiment in eastern France, the regiment in which I was born and reared. There were eight men in my platoon whom I had known since I was 14. It was an amazing coincidence.

I joined the regiment in Luxembourg. Three months later, in Germany, I was seriously wounded in Lambertsburg, west of the Rhine, in what turned out to be the last day of heavy fighting for our unit. I was evacuated to a hospital in Luxembourg for an initial operation, then evacuated by air to England for follow-up operations. I returned to New York on a hospital ship and was put on a hospital train to the Army General Hospital in Augusta, Georgia, where I spent three months recuperating.

I was reassigned back to the Cavalry School at Fort Riley, where I was asked whether I would like to become a pilot. I was to become a pilot in the Army, though trained for the task by the Air Force. I was reassigned to Germany in March 1947, and assigned once again to the 6th Cavalry, where I was to fly an L-5.

Shortly thereafter, I was chosen to be the aide of General Trudeau, commander of the First Constabulary Brigade at Wiesbaden. After six months with him, I was reassigned, in August 1949, to a position as company commander in the 3rd Battalion of the 14th Cavalry Regiment. Soon thereafter, I was reassigned to the 82nd Airborne Division. After about 60 days, I was selected for the advanced course in the armor school at Fort Knox, Kentucky. On the way, I got married. Two of my colleagues who had been similarly reassigned also married en route to Fort Knox.

The years 1950 and 1951 were spent at Fort Knox, where I was promoted to Captain, in command of D Company of the 1st Tank Battalion, 1st Armored Division. I was soon reassigned to the role of Aviation Operations Officer. In the Korean War, I served as pilot for the Corps Commander. But I also flew fixed-wing planes. I remember one day when I had a two-hour mission in a fixed-wing aircraft early in the morning, then returned to pilot a helicopter for the Corps Commander.

The Korean War ended in July 1953, and I was reassigned to the 7th Infantry Division, to serve as the executive officer of their Aviation Company. In 1954 I was reassigned to Fort Benning, Georgia as Commander of the Aviation Company of the 3rd Infantry Division. Two years later, I was reassigned, as a student, to the Command General Staff College at Fort Leavenworth, Kansas. After a year I was reassigned as an instructor at the college, with the rank of Major. At the same time, I leased a 160-acre farm, ten miles west of the post, and started up a beef cattle herd. The fourth and fifth of our six children were born at Fort Leavenworth.

While at both Benning and Leavenworth I was able to take college courses, which added up to three and a half years of college credit. When I was assigned to Germany in 1960, I was able to do what they called boot-strapping, a leave of absence without pay for further schooling. I got a bachelor's degree from the University of Nebraska in January 1961.

I was assigned as a staff officer to the US Army's European headquarters at Heidelberg, Germany. Now a Lieutenant Colonel, I served as Berlin Action Officer and as an Aviation Staff Officer. My family joined me, and for a year and a half the eight of us lived off base in a two-bedroom apartment. Our five oldest children shared what we called the "squad room," and the sixth child, who was born there, was with my wife and me.

The children were too young to go to school. They learned to speak German by playing with their neighbors. The oldest became fluent in the language.

After a year and a half, I was reassigned to the 2nd Squadron, 11th Cavalry at Landshut, on the Czech border. I was responsible for the southern forty miles of the Czech border, fronting three Czech divisions.

In September 1963, I was reassigned to the US Strike Command at McGill Air Force Base, in Tampa, Florida. We bought the home in which we still live, in St. Petersburg. After two years, I was reassigned to Vietnam, where I served for 16 months in the 1st Cavalry Division, as commander of the division support command, where I achieved the rank of Lieutenant Colonel, and later as Commander of the Air Cavalry Squadron.

In July 1967, I was assigned to the Army War College in Carlisle, Pennsylvania. Officers who weren't assigned to the War College were required to retire early. A War College assignment was a requirement for promotion to General. That was also true of the Air Force, and for admirals in the Navy.

I was not happy at the War College, and applied to go back to Vietnam. I learned that I was on the list for promotion to Brigadier General, but that would mean an assignment to the Pentagon, which I didn't want. So I asked a friend in the Pentagon to see to it that this didn't happen, so I could go back to Vietnam as a colonel. My wife has never forgiven me.

The Commanding General of the 1st Aviation Brigade, an old friend, met me at Tan Son Nhut Airport and escorted me to his command car. He told me he was assigning me to his Deputy slot, which carried the rank of Brigadier General.

Our command consisted of 27,000 troops and 2,100 aircraft, divided among 115 aviation companies. I spent the next eight months visiting Air Force units, and also the ground units we were supporting.

Then I was reassigned to the role of Deputy Division Commander of the 101st Airborne Division, in 1st Corps, where I spent 16 months, for a total of 24 months in the country. Most people were assigned there for only a year.

In July 1971, I was placed in command of the Fort Stewart Hunter Army Air Field at Fort Stewart, Georgia, part of the Army aviation flight training center. Eight months later I was promoted to Major General and assigned to command the First Armored Division at Fort Pitt, Texas. To my great surprise, General Palmer, the Vice Chief of Staff of the Army, who presided over the promotion ceremony, had brought my parents down from Washington with him. Three months later, I was given command of the First Cavalry Division, which was returning home from Vietnam.

After two years, I was reassigned to the role of Commander of a Readiness Regional Headquarters at Fort Sheridan, Illinois, overseeing the training of 100,000 soldiers in National Guard and Army Reserve units in the states of Illinois, Wisconsin, Minnesota, Iowa and Missouri.

Two years later, in 1975, I was assigned as Chief of Staff in a command center with the triple roles of 8th Army Headquarters; Headquarters, US Forces in Korea; and 8th Army Headquarters.

I was also assigned the role of spokesman at Panmunjom for the United States Armistice Commission, which meant that I conducted, for the US side, all talks at Panmunjom.

My next assignment was the command of the Army Aviation Center at Fort Rucker, Alabama. I stayed on at Panmunjom for three days to orient my replacement.

At Fort Rucker, I spent two and a half years, beginning in July 1976. Our task was training army pilots, army maintenance people, and so forth. In December 1979, the Vice Chief of Staff of the Army phoned me to say that everyone knew how reluctant I was to serve in the Pentagon, so he was chosen to break the bad news to me that I was to come to the Pentagon to become the Army's first Director of Training, that is, all the Army's training. Up to that point, training had been fragmented. I spent my last 2 1/2 years bringing those fragments together. I worked right up to my date of mandatory retirement, March 1, 1981.

HAROLD STETSON

I grew up in Bristol, Pennsylvania, a manufacturing center. I remember particularly the Fleetwing aircraft factory, which produced amphibians. My older brother enlisted in the Navy in 1941, and soon became an Aviation Machinist Mate, First Class. I tried to enlist at 17, but I was told to finish high school, which I did on June 6, 1944 (D-Day at Normandy). That summer I enlisted in the Navy in Philadelphia, and was assigned to Jacksonville, Florida.

Harold Stetson

Boot camp during a miserably hot summer in Florida was followed by training in Memphis, Tennessee as an aviation Radioman and Radarman. Then I went back to Cecil Field, near Jacksonville, for gunnery and other stuff, for about six weeks. I remember working with a 50-caliber machine gun—taking it down, cleaning it, and putting it back together. I was given my choice of service on a bomber or a seaplane. I chose the latter, knowing that it could land on water if necessary.

In March 1945, I was sent to a training squadron at Banana River, Florida, for training as a member of the crew of a VPB2, a patrol bomber. A part of our training was flying submarine patrols, but we never spotted one, because the Germans had no submarines left. We'd stop at the Guantanamo Bay base in Cuba, because we knew that was a good source for silk stockings, watches, and other luxuries in short supply.

With the war in Europe winding down, I was assigned to the West Coast. We traveled by train, and picked up new planes when we got there. Though the war ended in August, we continued to move west, first to Hawaii and then to Guam and Saipan, where we stayed for three or four months. Our mission was to rescue downed pilots, but we never actually did it. One thing we did do was transport USO girls.

We later moved to Ebai, near Kwajalein, in the Caroline Islands. One task was to drop dive bombs, so the German geophysicists (serving the Allied cause) could see the flow of the water. Our next task was to fly natives from Bikini to Rongelap, so we could use their home as a test site for an atomic bomb. We told them they would be home in two months or so. But 60 years later, they still haven't gone back.

From Saipan, I took two trips to Truk. After that, I was able to hitch a ride back to Hawaii, where I caught a ship to Treasure Island. After two or three days, I took a trip home to Maryland and was discharged.

With the help of a man at Rohm and Haas (they had given me a prize when I was in high school), I went to Penn State and graduated in 1950 with a degree in chemistry. In that depression year, jobs were scarce, so I applied for graduate school, and was accepted by both Penn State and Yale. Penn State also offered me a graduate assistantship, so I stayed on, and got a PhD in ceramics.

I started work at Corning Glass, and later went on to RCA and then Western Electric. The latter was then a subsidiary of AT&T.

I married in 1952, so this is our 50th anniversary. We had three children, a girl, now 49, and two guys, now 46 and 42.

I came to live in Newtown when I was working at RCA. My father had a car repair shop at Wrights and Eagle Roads. He offered to build a house for me if I would buy the raw materials. It was a beautiful house, a huge house. But we had no neighbors, no one for the kids to play with. So we went to George Ermentrout, a realtor, and he advertised it in the *Wall Street Journal*. He quickly got a buyer, who wanted to move in right away. George knew that Mrs. Watson wanted to sell her house, so we bought it, and have lived in it ever since. There is a beautiful copper beech, the last one in Newtown.

GEORGE STIEBER

I was born in Philadelphia, Pennsylvania on February 12, 1920. I was drafted on December 8, 1941. It was coincidental that I reported for duty the day after Pearl Harbor. I was sent to Fort Meade, Maryland for three days, and then to Fort Bragg, North Carolina for basic training in field artillery. When I finished my basic training, I was kept as an instructor. I taught enlisted men who were being screened to go to OCS, and teaching reserve officers, who were being recalled for active duty. I did that for several months, teaching them to drive ten-wheeled Diamond T trucks through the woods and swamps, and up and down the hills. I soon got bored with that. I saw a sign one day that said, "Join the Aviation Cadets." So I went over to Pope Field, took the test, and passed.

George Stieber

And from there, I went to Nashville, Tennessee for one week of psychological and physical testing. Then I was classified as a student pilot.

I went to Maxwell Field, Alabama, and taught a two-month course that was primarily for civilians brought into the program. After that, I went to flying school at Hawthorne in Orangeburg, South Carolina. You had to solo a minimum of ten hours, or you would wash out. I completed that two-month course of 65 hours flying time, and then I went to basic flying school at Bush Field, in Augusta, Georgia, for another 65 hours flying in a basic trainer, BT-13. Then I went to train at Turner Field in Albany, Georgia in an AT-9 and in the meantime, we were also learning to fly on instruments, in an AT-10.

I was lucky in the war. In the process of becoming an aviation cadet, one of the company clerks told me I had an IQ of 126. I think the fact

George Stieber

that I had that kind of an IQ resulted in my being retained as an instructor in the field artillery, and later as an instructor of the crews of B-17s and B-24s.

In the meantime, I was commissioned a 2nd Lieutenant. Then I went to Chanute Field, Illinois, to complete the necessary instruction and flying time in order to fly a B-17. Then I got checked out on a B-24. Then we received orders that they needed three instructor pilots to go to B-29s. We all had the required minimum of 500 hours of four-engine experience. We were sent to an operational training unit at Grand Island, Nebraska. This is a unit being formed, as opposed to a replacement training unit, where you are sent to replace those that got shot down. We trained as a whole group

together. We did a lot of training in Puerto Rico, not knowing at the time that we were going to be stationed on Guam. But it was a similar climate. We went back and forth to Puerto Rico two or three times. We had to fly three 3,000-mile missions. We were then sent overseas and got brand new airplanes.

We arrived late in the war. I flew only five or six bombing missions over Japan before the atomic bombs were dropped. Our missions took 14 hours or more. I flew one mission of 17 hours and 10 minutes. I think it was 3800 miles.

I was married in 1953 to Joanne, and have three children. Ruth, the oldest, was a special education teacher at Council Rock; she adopted two children; Mark isn't married; and Eric, a graduate of West Point in 1983, participated in the Gulf War, and has two children.

I was drafted on December 8, 1941 and discharged on December 1945, after four years in WW II.

After my discharge, I worked for a little while on several jobs as a carpenter and mechanic. I even tried farming for a while. Then I went to work for Lavelle Aircraft in Newtown for 15 years. I ended up as plant manager, until the plant closed down. Then I went to work at Saint Mary's Hospital for 18 years as director of plant operations. Then, in 1990, I retired on my 70th birthday. I was a township supervisor, and chairman of the Council Rock Health Council.

I enjoy gardening, and my neighbors benefit, by helping me to reap the harvest.

MALCOLM (MICKEY) SWAYNE

(as compiled by Kingdon Swayne)

Malcolm's story is sad and brief. He graduated from George School in 1944 and immediately joined the Navy, which sent him to New Guinea. There he simply disappeared in the fall of that year. He is honored among the missing in an American military cemetery in the Philippines. He is specially mourned by the author of this memoir, who was his roommate in the Swayne household for most of his life.

CLIFTON (TIP)WIGGINS

I was born on November 28, 1925, on a farm on Eagle Road, Newtown, Pennsylvania. I attended the Chancellor Street School in Newtown, and was supposed to graduate in June of 1944. At that time, all grades attended the Chancellor Street School. On January 1, 1944, I enlisted in the United States Navy. I went to the school principal, Dr. Nagley, and asked "Will I get my diploma if I enlist in the Navy?" He said, "I'll have to take it up with the school board." Two weeks later he came back and said, "Yeah, you'll get your diploma." I was out in the Pacific when my mother picked up my diploma.

I was sent to Sampson, New York for my boot camp training. No sooner had we arrived at the base than they made us run around a track carrying heavy lug-

Clifton Wiggins

gage. All the people that had office jobs were really hurting. For me, I was in great shape. I used to run three miles to school every day. The other guys were winded. So after 21 days, I was sent to gunnery school in Rhode Island. While in gunnery school, we slept in hammocks for 16 weeks. Then, they sent me to Florida. We stayed in a hotel on Biscayne Boulevard, where we had full-size beds. I was sent to Charleston, South Carolina to pick up a ship, the *USS Converse* DD 509. Only three were built. It was built on a destroyer's hull, only 150 feet long, with lots of fire power and capability to deploy depth charges. After passing through the Panama Canal, we stopped briefly along the Mexican Coast, at Manzanilla. At three o'clock in the morning, we got run out, because so many of the crew were drunk from drinking tequila. We stopped briefly again at San Diego, and then Pearl Harbor, and from there on out into the far Pacific, with a short stop at Eniwetok.

I served two years and six months in the Navy on three different vessels: the *USS Gunboat PGM 17*, the *USS Converse* DD 509, and the *USS Intrigue*, a mine sweeper. I was discharged as a gunner's mate, GM 2/c.

In 1949, I married Betty Hickey of Langhorne. We have three children, two daughters and one son.

I owned and operated a car repair shop in Newtown for 32 years.

In my retirement, I like to work in the garden, and my wife and I like to travel and go to places that have activities for retirees.

I came from a big family of 12 children: five boys and seven girls. My parents were William Wiggins Wiggins and Laura Randall Wiggins.

Four of the five boys served in the Navy during World War II, the other boy, Stanley, a twin, stayed at home and ran the farm.

Sam was a US Navy electrician's mate assigned to Camp Perry, Virginia. He is married with two children.

Bill was a US Navy electrician's mate for six years stationed at Norfolk, Virginia. Before Bill got out, he enjoyed a world cruise aboard the cruiser *USS Helena*. Bill is married with four children.

Sam Wiggins

John was assigned to a US Navy gun crew in the Merchant Marine. John is married with two girls.

Clifton (Tip) served aboard three different Navy vessels: *USS Converse*, DD509, a destroyer; and *USS PGM17*, a gunboat; and the *USS Intrigue*, a minesweeper.

The girls in the order that they were born were: Anna Jane, Leanora, Ruth Elaine, Madeline June, Iverna Reba, Mildred Catherine, and Helen Shirley.

Bill Wiggins

John Wiggins

ALLAN WINN

Allan Winn

I was born in 1912 in Pusan, Korea, of missionary parents, who taught me at home. I went to high school and college in Emporia, Kansas, and from there to Princeton Seminary. While there I drove each Sunday down to the shore to lead a church service. At the time Betty was a student at Princeton Music College. I saw her picture in a photographer's show window, and sought her out. Betty and I were married in 1938; I graduated from Divinity School in 1939, and began my service in the ministry at Merrick, Long Island, followed by an assignment to Reading, Pennsylvania. In 1941 I enlisted in the Navy and learned the ropes at a school for Navy chaplains in Norfolk, Virginia before being commissioned as a Navy chaplain. I was then assigned to Brooklyn, New York in 1942, serving a number of ships as a chaplain conducting religious services and performing other responsibilities. There was a naval hospital there, where I spent most of the time assisting in the needs of returning wounded war veterans.

During the war, one of the places we stayed for a while was Greenwich Village, in an 8-story walk-up apartment, and I drove back and forth to the naval base. My office was on the second floor of a building at the entrance of the Navy Yard. I had an assistant, a Presbyterian minister from Missouri named Walter. He was just out of Divinity School, a very fine man. One of our duties was to assist in commissioning ships, along with the lady who wielded the champagne bottle. I believe I participated in the commissioning of more than 100 ships. At that time the Chaplain's office would present to the Ship's captain a Holy Bible, more than likely with the inscription " Presented to the *USS LSM 215* on 23 July 1944 at the time of her commissioning. The Chaplain's Office extends its good wishes to the officers and men on 23 July 1944."

On some Sundays I put my assistant in charge of the church service on the naval base and, for my own pleasure, attended the service at the Fifth Avenue Presbyterian Church.

There was a male quartet, calling themselves the Mariners, who sang at our church service every Sunday. Our service was broadcast, and the group became very well known. After the war, when I had a church in Trenton, they came down for a Sunday service.

My next assignment was to a unit in Maine, a Construction Battalion of the 103 Seabees, which shortly thereafter moved to Seattle. Our unit traveled across the country on two trains, with the commanding officer in charge of one, while I was in charge of the other. They were skilled carpenters, with some good musicians among them. We were assigned to a brand new vessel, an APA troop ship, the *St. Croix*, commissioned in Seattle. Our next stop was San Diego. From there we headed across the Pacific to the Philippines.

After the war I continued my service in the Navy and the Marine Corps reserves for 20 years, and retired as a Commander.

Following World War II, I was called as pastor of the Third Presbyterian Church of Trenton, which merged with Fifth and Mt. Carmel Churches to form Covenant Presbyterian Church. I helped build the church at Parkway and Parkside Avenues in Trenton, New Jersey and continued there until my retirement in 1974.

I held many state and national positions in the Presbyterian Church, and was an active member of Rotary International, American Legion, the boards of Trenton's Council of Social Agencies, and Bloomfield College.

In 1969, I received an honorary Doctor of Divinity degree from Bloomfield College.

I retired from Covenant Presbyterian Church in Trenton, New Jersey, in 1974.

After my retirement, I returned to Newtown to live in the house where my wife was born and raised. I also was interim pastor at many churches, such as in Newtown, Chester, Dutch Neck, Willingboro, Flemington, and Hopewell.

Compiler's Note:

The following are stories recently told to the author by Al Winn's daughter, Barbara Winn:

There was a story about my dad while they were stationed at a training base in Maine. They'd been stationed there for a couple of months, waiting to know where they'd be serving. Orders came through late on a Friday sending them overseas Sunday, or early Monday. "All the Brass," as Dad would call them, had already gone home, or went home at this point without giving orders for any leave – so the boys were stuck there, about to go to war without saying goodbye to their loved ones. Dad was the only officer left, and he quickly felt responsible for the dilemma. He flagged an MP riding a motorcycle with a side-car, and had him drive to the nearest bank. On entering the bank, he demanded lots of cash (in the name of the US Navy!), and signed a statement so that his troops could go home on a weekend pass to say good-bye to their loved ones before " shipping out." He raced back to the base with the money, and immediately set up a table and chair for himself, lined the men up, and doled out enough money so that each man could go home for the weekend. When the superior officers found out about it, Dad was called on the carpet for his overly enterprising efforts, but they finally realized there wasn't much they could do about it after the fact, and I don't think he lost any stripes over it. Even if he had, I'm sure he would have said it was worth it. I've always loved his heroic, slightly mischievous, friend-of-the-common-man image.

There's also the story from his days in the Brooklyn Navy Yard. My dad had set up his "office" – a table and chair – right inside the door of the main compound, so anyone coming or going had to pass him. Good marketing, no? A young woman came in carrying an infant and looking for a particular sailor named Joe. Dad obligingly went off to find him for her, but when they came back, only the baby was there. A note pinned to the baby's clothes read, "Joe, YOU take him for awhile." I think Joe's parents had to raise the child, since Joe couldn't very well take him along to the war! On the other hand, I can sympathize with the girl.

BOB BARNETT

Bob Barnett

I was born on October 13, 1924 in Philadelphia, Pennsylvania. I attended Olney High School, but I didn't graduate, because the war came along and I was anxious to enlist before I was drafted, so I enlisted in the US Coast Guard. I served from December 1, 1942 until I got a medical discharge on August 1, 1944. I found out about this program through a business partner of my father's, who was a Navy Commander. He thought I might be interested in a dog training program with the US Coast Guard, since I had so much interest and experience with dogs. He said that the Coast Guard had openings in a dog training program. I was eligible for the draft, so I enlisted in the US Coast Guard. I was given no formal military training, no boot camp. They just issued me a uniform and told me to report for my first assignment, which was training German Shepherds and Doberman Pinschers, at Melrose Park, Pennsylvania, just outside Philadelphia.

A man by the name of "Pab" Weidner from Melrose Park (Elkins Park), a horse fancier who raised racing horses, donated his entire estate, stables and all, including a train station, to the US Coast Guard. I worked there for three months, training dogs for sentry and coastal patrol work. At that time there were about 200 dogs.

Many of the dogs came from private individuals, with the understanding that they would be returned to the owner after the war. Puppies born to dogs that were bred during confinement or training would be loaned to a volunteer until the dog was a year old, returned for training, and then sent out on the job.

There were dog trainers and dog fanciers that contributed a great deal to the training program. The dogs were trained to attack on command and smell or sniff for special, identifiable objects.

I trained sentry dogs, and used the same for beach patrol work. The Coast Guard patrolled beaches from Maine to Florida, and provided guard duty at various installations along the Atlantic Coast, for both the Army and Navy. My first patrol duty was from Townsend Inlet (Strathmere) to Sea Isle City, New Jersey. Later I was assigned to the First Naval District in Boston, at South Weymouth, Massachusetts, and then to Boston, Massachusetts, guarding installations like the

Naval Air Station-hangers, and Boston Harbor. It was from here that many of the Navy Blimps, used in combatting the German submarines, were berthed.

Then I was transferred to Boston proper, to the transportation division of the Coast Guard, driving ambulances from ships to shore bases. Dogs were used on all government installations, mostly for coastal patrol. Both the Marine Corps and the Army used them overseas.

The Army, at Front Royal, Virginia had a dog training school there and most of the dogs were used overseas in combat situations. The Army and Coast Guard collaborated, training sentry dogs which were sent all over the world for sentry duty.

After my return home from the service, I worked for 21 years for Erwin Chevrolet in Philadelphia, selling cars. I left there, and with two of my high school buddies, set up a car dealership for ten years. After that, I struck out on my own, and bought, repaired and sold cars. I still like to tinker with cars.

I was married in 1944 and have three children, two girls and a boy. I have lived in Newtown for the past 25 years.

SAM CRAIGHEAD
(as compiled by Bill Craighead)

Sam Craighead

Samuel Eby Craighead was born on March 8, 1919 in St. Petersburg, Florida. He finished high school at George School, Newtown, Pennsylvania in 1937, and graduated from Penn State University in 1941. Being immediately subject to the military draft, he was required to report but was turned down, classified 4-F, (physically unfit for military service). There wasn't anything further from the truth. He was in perfect physical condition, but according to military standards he was too small, under the prescribed height and weight. His desire was to get in the Air Force, and be a tail-gunner on a B-17. If he knew then what I have learned since, I'm sure he would have thought otherwise. I don't know how true it is, but I have heard that the average life of a tail-gunner aboard a B-17 was 13 minutes.

My brother tried different ways to get into the war. He was called up for seven of the eight drafts, every six months, but was turned down, to his immense disappointment. Finally, they didn't call him for the final draft.

Right after college, he got a job with the Federal Government and the Geological Survey in Harrisburg, Pennsylvania. During WW II he spent two-and-a-half years in Alaska with the US Geodetic Survey, and when the war ended he was in Alabama. Just after the war, he returned to Harrisburg, Pennsylvania, where he continued to work for the Federal Government until his retirement.

He told me on occasions the ridicule he had to endure because he was not in WW II, which was most unpleasant. He hated it, and it was always a disappointment for him that he had not served in the war.

He married Janet Strong from Harrisburg, Pennsylvania in 1947. They had two daughters, Laurie and Patti, and five grandchildren. He died in 1984 while living in Boiling Springs, and is buried in Carlisle, Pennsylvania.

He was quite a musician, and loved to play many of the woodwind instruments. He would play classical music with his flute, accompanied by his mother on the piano. He played a piccolo in the Penn State band, and enjoyed playing an assortment of woodwind instruments to accompany Lawrence Welk's band on Saturday night TV. Sometimes he would even play at the local bar.

M. J. DONOVAN

M.J. Donovan

Iwas born on November 1, 1925, in Newtown, Pennsylvania. I went to parochial school in my earlier years, and then to Newtown High School, formerly called the Chancellor Street School. I left high school in my junior year. This was during some of the most crucial fighting in WW II. So that I wouldn't be drafted, and possibly end up in the Army, I chose to enlist in the US Coast Guard, which I did on October 8, 1943.

I left Newtown Station on the Reading Line, and went to the recruiting station in Philadelphia. From the recruiting station, we went to the Broad Street Station in Philadelphia, where twelve of us boarded a train for Penn Station in New York City. After lunch, we boarded a Coast Guard truck, and were transported to Manhattan Beach Training Station at Sheep's Head Bay.

The man in charge of our physical fitness program was none other than the famous prize fighter, Lieutenant Commander Jack Dempsey.

We finished boot camp in the middle of January 1944, and then had a 10-day leave. On our return from our leave, we laid around for about two weeks, and then were sent to the receiving station at Little Creek, Virginia. I was transported to Captain of the Port, Baltimore, Maryland (5th Coast Guard District). I was there for three months, assigned to picket boat duty. After that I was assigned to the US Navy Mine Warfare Test Station at Solomons, Maryland. While there, we patrolled a restricted area on an 83-footer. Then I was briefly on air-sea rescue patrol. One of our boats was like a PT boat. The US Coast Guard earlier was involved in patrolling and protecting the seaport. It was in '42 and '43 that the German submarines were a menace to our shipping en route to Europe. By late 1943 and 1944, submarine warfare was brought under control. However, I was not involved in that earlier activity.

When the war in Europe was over, I was still aboard the 83-footer, stationed at the United States Mine Warfare Test Station at Solomons, Maryland, where they tested mines and torpedoes. Some of my patrol duty was on a Coast Guard 83-footer. Because most of this area was restricted, the Coast Guard was given the duty of patrolling it. Most of my time in the Coast Guard was spent there. Just before I was discharged, I spent some time at the Navy Yard in Washington D.C.

At this time, the US Coast Guard spent a lot of time patrolling and protecting our seaports along both the Atlantic and the Pacific Coast. I participated in some of that kind of duty, but I was not in any actual combat. I was discharged from the US Coast Guard on May 21, 1946.

In 1950, I started working for General Motors, the Ternstedt Division, Fischer Body. They made automotive hardware. During WW II, they made torpedo bombers. This was an assembly plant, with parts coming from Tarrytown, New York; Wilmington, Delaware; and Baltimore, Maryland.

During the 38 years I was there, we made automotive hardware for GM cars and trucks. At one point, I became supervisor of quality standards.

Since I retired in 1988 from General Motors in Trenton, New Jersey, I have been active with the Morrell Smith, American Legion Post #440, in Newtown, and the Newtown Historical Association, gathering and assembling information on veterans from the different wars, including WW I, for the records, archives, and displays for special events.

I have compiled a lot of pictures of veterans of WW II, and displayed them at various functions here in Newtown, including Memorial Day. These pictures are on file with the Newtown Historical Society. I have titled this display of pictures, "1941 Reflections of World War II, 1945."

Another project I helped with was when the Pennsylvania State Legislature approved awarding a high school diploma to any veteran of WW II, who had left school early. The project was called "Operation Recognition." On November 11, 2001, 34 veterans from Newtown High School were awarded a high school diploma by the superintendent of the Council Rock School District, Tim Kirby. I am proud to say that I am one of the recipients of a diploma.

Another project, which I am very proud of, is the memorial for those graduates of Newtown High School who were killed during WW II. A display case now appears in the Chancellor Street Center in Newtown, in their honor. It is now an office building for the administrative staff of the Council Rock School System. This honor roll memorializes their names, a brief description of their service, and a photograph. Family members were there to receive the plaque for each veteran. There were eleven men from Newtown High School honored posthumously, on May 21, 2005, who gave their lives for their country.

They are as follows:

Cahill, Robert J.	Army	November 20, 1944
Dutton, George F.	Army A.F.	September 11, 1943
Hennessey, George F.	Army	November 8, 1944

Hennessey, Leon M.	Army	March 13,1945
Hilsee, Marvin H.	Army	August 1, 1944
Kirby, Varsal	Army	June 7,1944
Maher, Edward L.	Army	March 24, 1944
Murfit Jr., Wallace G.	Army A.F.	August 1, 1945
Strathie, Arthur R.	Army A. F.	March 11,1944
Swayze, William H.	Army	April 28, 1945
Van Artsdalen, Clifford C.	Army	June 5, 1945

In 1960 I married an art teacher from the Pennsbury school system by the name of Josephine Schera. We have two children, a boy and a girl.

JUNE FULTON
(wife of Chuck Fulton)

I was born on June 22, 1925 in Lebanon, Pennsylvania. When I was one year old, my parents moved to the Lehigh Valley, Northampton County region of Pennsylvania. I attended public school, first to third grades in Bangor and third to ninth in Bath. The nearest high school was in Nazareth and as there was no school bus program, I commuted there by public transportation, which cost about $3 per month. I graduated in June 1943 and started nurse's training at Allentown Hospital, Allentown, Pennsylvania.

Chuck and June Fulton

As WWII progressed, more and more registered nurses joined the Armed Services, and a nationwide shortage of nurses for civilian hospitals developed. In response Congress established the Cadet Nurse Corp under the Department of Public Health Service. It would pay tuition and room and board as you studied and trained to become a nurse. This was in exchange for a commitment to work in the Public Health Services upon graduation. The commitment was for as long as the war was going on.

I thus became a Cadet Nurse, but the war was over by the time I graduated in June 1946 and the Cadet Nurse Corp Program had ended. However, since there was still a severe nurse shortage, by request of the Director of Nursing, I stayed at Allentown Hospital for one more year. I subsequently worked for a cardiologist at Cornell University Hospital in NYC, and as a school nurse in the Southern Lehigh County.

TOM HALLOWELL

In 1915 I was born in Baltimore, Maryland, and spent my childhood and youth in Sandy Spring, Maryland, living on three different farms in the community. When I was four years old, my father died, a traumatic event in my life.

In 1930, I went to George School, Bucks County, Pennsylvania, for an excellent secondary school education, along with great experiences in sports and influences from fine people. Swarthmore College followed. I graduated in 1937 with high honors in chemistry, which led to a PhD in organic chemistry from Massachusetts Institute of Technology in 1940. That August I started work with the DuPont Company at their Experimental Station in Wilmington, Delaware, where I did research on making nylon accept color dyes.

Tom Hallowell

Europe was involved with World War II, and war seemed likely for the USA. Due to major influences from my Quaker backgound -- forebears, parents, home community, secondary school, and college, I signed up with the draft board as a CO (Conscientious Objector).

After Pearl Harbor on December 7, 1941, many DuPont chemists were exempt from the draft because they were working on projects important to the military. For example, one project I worked on was creating a military uniform resistant to poison gas and another involved research on chemicals suitable for insect repellents. So secret was our work that we were often unaware what project chemists in the adjacent labs were working on. We chemists felt we were contributing a satisfying share to the war effort, and, of course, we did various war-related jobs in the community, too.

A memorable wartime challenge involved my assistance to a wonderful family recently and prematurely bereft of a father. I had made my home with them for several years as if part of the family. I was home one evening when a telegram arrived from the War Department stating that their 19-year-old son had been killed while fighting with General Patton's forces in Germany. Though not personal battlefield trauma, the impact of this second tragedy certainly involved me in a wartime experience caused by it.

In 1946, DuPont transferred me to its Photo Products plant in Parlin, New Jersey, where I did research on color photographic film and films for a wide variety of industrial and graphic arts uses. During the ensuing years, I married, had three children, and enjoyed living close to the NJ Atlantic Coast.

In 1971, DuPont transferred me to the North Carolina mountains, where they had a plant for producing medical x-ray film. I was in charge of planning a research laboratory building for it.

In early 1979, with the new lab built, staffed, and running well and nearly 39 years at DuPont behind me, and with the children well along in their education, I retired. My wife and I promptly took a two-month camping trip to the Southwest, and settled home later with a whole new life ahead. Adventure travel rated high, plus hiking and trail maintenance in the National Forests of the mountains, a lot of nature and conservation work, Boy Scouts, photography, and eventually, eleven grandchildren. I now live in a retirement community near my wife's hometown of Kennett Square, Pennsylvania, and hit 90 years in October, 2005.

Amid these many years, the war years stand out as a special time. Our country pulled together with remarkable unity. It underwent shortages and inconveniences with patience and without complaint. Those years were not pleasant ones. Heartbreak came frequently and required help, but we all persevered and learned, whether by fighting abroad or keeping the home front intact.

BILL HAYMAN
(as recounted by his wife, Marion)

On Pearl Harbor day, Bill and I were returning from Galeton, Pennsylvania to Philadelphia, where we lived. Our visit to Galeton was to prepare for our wedding, on January 1.

At the time, Bill was working for Smith, Kline and French, manufacturers of pharmaceuticals, as assistant to the director of manufacturing. The firm's work supported the war effort.

The company applied for a deferment, which they had to do every six months. It was granted, and he was deferred for the entire war. His working hours, without overtime pay, were 7:00 to 4:00 and 6:00 to 11:00.

After the war, Bill became a purchasing agent for the same company.

Bill and Marion Hayman

When the Korean War came along, Bill's brother was called into the service, and Bill replaced him in the family pharmacy in Galeton, Pennsylvania. But Bill was anxious to get back into industry, so he signed on with Burroughs Wellcome, as chief pharmacist. He stayed with them until he retired in 1981.

At about that time, he took a group of six young men to the Philippines on a work-study exchange sponsored by Rotary. There he became acquainted with the International Executive Service Corps (IESC). When he returned home, he signed on as a volunteer for IESC. In that role, he traveled, with me by his side, to Panama, Ecuador, Indonesia, Kenya, Egypt, Jordan, El Salvador, and Thailand. We returned a second time to some of these countries.

Our older son, Bill, is a physician. He has served as a ship's doctor, and also in Bolivia and Switzerland. Emergency medicine is his specialty. He is now engaged mostly in administrative tasks, getting new hospitals for the emergency room group, hiring physicians for them, and solving problems that come along.

David, our younger son, is also a doctor. During his college days, he worked on the hospital ship HOPE in Tunisia and Brazil. After graduation from medical school, while waiting for a position with the Center for Disease Control (CDC) in Atlanta, he worked in Prudhoe Bay, Guatemala, and on a Coast Guard ice breaker in the Antarctic. His work with CDC took him to India, Sierra Leone, the Ivory Coast, Cameroon, and especially Malawi in Africa. He is presently employed by the World Health Organization (WHO) in their office in Geneva. He is now one of the nine directors of WHO, and deals mostly with communicable viral diseases including Ebola virus, malaria and polio.

My husband and I were able to visit David in Africa many times.

EILEEN LANCASTER

Eileen Lancaster

I was born on April 23, 1927, the same day as the childhood movie star, Shirley Temple. I grew up in Fox Chase, and went to St. Cecilia's grammar school there. I then graduated in the first class at St Hubert's High School in 1944.

I always wanted to be a nurse. Things were difficult just before and during World War II. President Roosevelt even considered drafting women for military service and training them to be nurses. It was then that the Army Cadet Nurse Corps was born. The government agreed to pay any person who signed up for the nursing program their tuition, room and board, and a small monthly allotment, and an army nurse's uniform, if they agreed to serve in the Army Nurse Corps after graduating from nursing school. Fortunately, enough nurses signed up, making it unnecessary to institute the drafting of nurses. This seemed like a good opportunity to satisfy my desire to become a nurse at very little cost to me, and to help the war effort, so I registered for the Army Cadet Nursing Program. We had to sign a paper at the time we registered, that we would agree to go into the armed service as a nurse, as soon as we graduated from nursing school. No ifs or buts. They gave us $15 a month while we were in nursing school and in the last six months they raised it to $30 a month.

Along with class work, we spent a lot of time taking care of patients in hospitals. The school was run by Sisters of Charity, the ones with the big hats.

In our free time, many evenings were spent walking from 16th and Girard to center city Philadelphia, and because we wore our army nurses uniform, they would let us in the big time movies for a quarter. Then, on our way back to our living quarters, we would stop in at the White Tower and get a hamburger for 15 cents and a soda for 10 cents. A big night on the town for 50 cents was often our entertainment.

I loved every minute of nursing school. There were 42 in our graduating class, including two men. We graduated in 1947, and because the war had ended, we didn't have to go into the service. However, some of our graduates still became Army nurses. I've worked in operating rooms and various duties in hospitals, but I have enjoyed most of all my time working in the field of psychiatry, especially working with young children. I've worked hard all my life, and eventually I became Director of Nursing at the Eastern State Hospital in Northeast Philadelphia, and am especially proud of that accomplishment.

Eileen Lancaster

The government took a long time before treating us as veterans of World War II. Many other services where men, and some women, were in training programs, received veterans' status. It was the Reagan administration that finally rewarded us with veterans' status. The facts that the government paid for our training and we signed an agreement to enter the military as an army nurse when we graduated from training carried a lot of weight. The result was that we are now considered veterans of World War II. When I came home, I immediately became a member of the American Legion in Newtown, Post #440.

For 30 years I was a resident of Yardley, Pennsylvania, but have been a resident of Newtown since 1987, and am presently a resident of the Pickering Manor Home, here in Newtown.

While in the Yardley area, my husband and I bought five acres and raised eight horses. We loved to ride, and did so almost every day.

My husband was in the Navy in WW II, and served aboard an LST (Landing Ship Tank) in the South Pacific. He became a Chief Petty Officer. We were married after he served his six years. We have two daughters, whom I love dearly, who visit me frequently. There are also six grandchildren.

Eileen Lancaster, Cadet Nurse

While in nursing school, many of us became lasting friends, and have met for lunch about once a month since graduating from nursing school. Our group is getting smaller, but after almost 60 years, some of us still get together.

I can still remember the day that Pearl Harbor was attacked. It was on a Sunday, and on the following Monday I went past places where you could enlist. The lines were out the doorway, and even around the block. There'll never be patriotism like that again.

PEARL MORRELL

Pearl Morrell

I was born in Panama on September 27, 1914. My mother and father met there during the construction of the Panama Canal, and were married in 1913. My mother was a nurse working for the Panama Canal Commission, and my father was working for the Navy in charge of the radio station in the jungle on Gatun Lake.

My father was a sailor in the American Navy at the age of 14, in the early years of the 20th century. Starting as an apprentice seaman, his first assignment was on the sailing vessel Hartford, where his station was at the top of the mast. At the beginning of World War II, he and I were both stationed in Philadelphia. Remarkably, both of us had the same rank -- Lieutenant Junior Grade. He retired shortly after the end of the war, and soon thereafter was called back into the service as a Chief Warrant Officer.

I wanted to join the Navy; I was finally able to do so in April 1943. My basic training was at Mt. Holyoke College in Massachusetts, followed by training in communications at Smith College.

My first assignment to duty, in July 1943, was at the headquarters of the 13th Naval District in Seattle. For the first few weeks, we lived with local residents while waiting for our quarters to be built, right on Puget Sound. Our workplace was at the Exchange Building in downtown Seattle, which had been taken over by the Navy. Our main task was to receive and redirect to the right place coded messages from ships at sea and land stations, both in the United States and abroad. We changed the codes regularly, about once a month, burning the parts of the old code that had been deleted.

We also trained communications officers for ships that were being outfitted, either in Seattle or in Bellingham, nearby. We were housed in comfortable living quarters. We were also trained in the use of .38 and .45 revolvers. My experience as a librarian enabled me to identify publications from civilian sources that would be of help to us. We also had access to publications from the Navy's Hydrographic Office, which we could consult if we received radio messages that we couldn't understand.

The people of Seattle were very kind to us. We could borrow books from the libraries, and works of art from their museums. We were welcomed into their churches. Those of us who were singers were invited to join a church choir that performed Handel's *Messiah* at Christmas time.

Early in March 1945, both my father and I were assigned to the Philadelphia Navy Yard. When I was given the task of writing a history of the 4th Naval Communications Office, he was of tremendous help to me, because he knew so much about the early years.

Perhaps the funniest thing that I ever had happen to me was when I had to deliver a radio message to a French submarine berthed in the Philadelphia Navy Yard. I was escorted by a Navy man, and was warned not to go below on that French submarine. Luckily, I didn't have to go below.

The Reserve Officer in charge of the Communications Office was a senseless tyrant. He made the Waves serve erratic shifts, and most of the girls ended up in sickbay. At this point, the war in Europe came to an end. I believed it was possible to cut back our number of telephones, from 12 to 8. But I could find no one willing to give up her or his telephone.

When I was discharged at the end of the war, my father (Herman Morrell) and I had the same rank (2nd Lieutenant). At the end of the war, we worked together doing archival work at the Philadelphia Navy Yard. On March 9, 1945 I was "promoted" into marriage.

ELIZABETH POWELL

I was born November 18, 1921 in Hamilton, Ohio, and graduated from the Northfield School for Girls in Northfield, Massachusetts. After graduating from high school, I was attending the Chouinard Art Institute in Los Angeles, California when Pearl Harbor was bombed. We immediately felt very vulnerable, with no Pacific fleet between Los Angeles and Japan. In less than a week, every instructor at the art school had signed up to do camouflage for all the aircraft factories around there.

Elizabeth Powell

As a result, I didn't see any sense in going to school with no instruction, so I quit, and got myself a job being a riveter at McDonald-Douglas Aircraft, riveting on the DC-3s. Working the "Swing shift" was a tough act. After three months I developed a herniated disc from bowling, which incapacitated me for a year and a half. When I felt good enough to be up and around again, I took a course in radio, and got my ham radio operator's license. During this time a Navy recruiter talked to us, and convinced me to join the WAVES (Women Accepted for Volunteer Emergency Service).

I came from a family that was very Army-oriented. My great grandfather was General Oliver Otis Howard, who founded Howard University. His sons had all been Army officers. So I joined the WAVES.

After six weeks of boot camp, the Navy sent six of us to Norfolk Naval Air Station. We were the first WAVES on the base, and housed in standard military barracks. There was an old Chief Petty Officer, Chief Mike, who lined up all the men, the enlisted men, and gave them the what for. He said he didn't think the women ought to be here, and he was worried that the men would get too friendly. It was a long time before we could get a conversation going with the men.

It was a large radio and radar repair base. When an aircraft carrier would come in, they would yank off every piece of equipment and send it to us for cleaning and repair. Sometimes we were over our heads in work, and sometimes we weren't. The Navy wanted to be sure each piece of equipment was working properly. We had electronic benches to which we could plug in each piece of equipment, set the dials, and see how the current was flowing. Though it was very boring work, it was essential, and there was a great deal of satisfaction, knowing we were helping the war effort.

When Japan surrendered in September 1945, we were discharged immediately. After almost two years in the Navy, I came home to Portland, Oregon. I took full advantage of the GI Bill of Rights and registered for a college education at Reed College, because at the time I couldn't get into an art school. There I received a very fine education.

All the first and second year students take a course in humanities. They teach history, the arts, and even music, and all about the country. Students break down for discussion into small groups of no more than 15. You know you have done your reading and you write papers. The woman professor who chaired our group said that all the teachers loved these groups with the GI's. You couldn't get away with anything. You mentioned something, and somebody would say, "Why do you say that?" The GI's were there to take advantage of a free education that they had so deservedly earned.

I left Reed College because I wanted to become an illustrator, so I came to New York and entered an art school there. Since art work was becoming more mechanical, my family thought I ought to try teaching, so I got a part-time job at a small private school, and also attended Columbia University part time.

After attending several colleges and working at various kinds of work, including teaching, I finally received a Bachelor of Fine Arts degree from Alfred University in the State of New York.

The most active part of my working career included some teaching, and then working for Stangl Pottery in Flemington, New Jersey as a ceramic designer, with some responsibility as a supervisor of the women glazing pottery.

Quite by accident, I ran into an old Quaker friend who told me that there was an opening in the Fine Arts Department at George School, in Newtown, Pennsylvania. I applied for the position and got the job. I started in 1961, and worked there for 25 years. Most of my time at George School was spent teaching ceramics. For five years, while still teaching ceramics and art, I was also responsible for a student cooperative work program.

My first one-woman show of my paintings was in Portland, Oregon, just after World War II. Since then, I have had a few one-woman shows in New York and Bucks County, as well as many group shows. In addition to ceramics and painting, I like to write and have had some of my writing published in professional magazines.

From one of her associates for many years at George School:
"Betty had a broad range of knowledge as well as a broad range of abilities."

Mercer Museum aficionados will know her books in the "Tools of the Nation Maker" series. Betty did one booklet on butter-making tools and on the tools used to make early Pennsylvania pottery. She also wrote articles for educational journals including, "What do you get from making pottery, besides a pot?" She had an upbeat and 'can do' attitude which was contagious to friends and family. Her beautifully decorated wheel-thrown pottery can be found in many homes in Bucks County and elsewhere. Her sister says, "Betty was a very caring person, and took special interest in younger members of her family."

Compilers Note:

Elizabeth A. Powell died before her account for this book could be published.

JOHN STREETZ

I was born August 18, 1926 in Salem, New Jersey: a town in South Jersey known for it's Quaker heritage, early glass factories, and being the birth place of the tomato industry in the USA.

I attended the Salem public schools; graduating from Salem High School in June of 1943.

I went to Lincoln University in September of 1943. This school is the oldest Institute of higher learning (1854) for African-Americans in the United States. After completing my senior year, I volunteered for the Army Air Corps Cadet Program that had been set up to develop a cadre of African airmen to serve in the then segregated army--the Tuskegee Airmen.

I took my basic training at Keeler Airfield, Biloxi, Mississippi, after which I was transferred to the Amarillo Air Base for four months

John Streetz and Bill Craighead

John Streetz Jackie Streetz and Bill Craighead

to study multi-engined aircraft mechanics. Later I was transferred to the North America Aviation factory at Anglo, California to learn the specifics of the B.B.C. medium bombers. The government was preparing a second group of Tuskegee airmen crews to serve in the Far East as squadrons of medium range support bombers. I finished that program as the crew chief of a group of 25, and prepared to go overseas. Just as we were ready to form up at the Tuskegee Air Base, the atomic bombs were dropped and the war ended.

After stints in Arizona and Oklahoma, I returned to Tuskegee, working on line maintaining the squadron's planes and participating in cross-country maneuvers until being discharged in August 1946. I returned to Lincoln University, graduating in June 1949 with majors in chemistry and biology.

After graduation, I taught at the Media Friends School in Pennsylvania. In 1950 I went to George School, in Newtown, Pennsylvania for sixteen years, taught chemistry and biology, and also served as a coach and dean of boys. My next position was as assistant headmaster and headmaster at Oakwood School in

Poughkeepsie, New York. I also served as Headmaster at the Athenian School in Danville, CA for two years. In 1970 I became the vice rresident for student affairs at California College of Arts and Crafts in Oakland, California. I remained there until 1985 when I became co-owner of a restaurant in Oakland, California and retired in 2000.

I have since been involved in service work at George School and the Fred Finch Center here in Oakland, and enjoyed long postponed travel -- 27 countries in the last five years.

During my stay in California I was briefly married to Erma Cox (two and a half years) we had one child, Reginald D. Streetz. In September of 1950, Jacqueline Moore and I were married and have one child, a daughter, Pamela Streetz.

KENNETH SWAYNE

(as compiled by Kingdon Swayne)

Kenneth Swayne

Kenneth graduated from George School in 1940, and undertook an accelerated war-time program at Lehigh University, where he graduated in 1943. His first job was at Oak Ridge, Tennessee, where he was a member of the team working on the atomic bomb. He was there for perhaps a year and a half, when someone in authority decided that the program should be required to give up some of its younger scientists to avoid charges of elitism. He spent the last six months of the war as an ordinary seaman in the Navy, stationed in Mississippi. He never quite got reconciled to what he regarded as a waste of his technical skills.

At the end of the war he returned to the family home at George School, where he soon got acquainted with Carol Frazee, one of the young teachers. He also signed on as a physicist for the Dupont Chemical Company, in Wilmington, Delaware. He and Carol married and set up housekeeping in Hockessin, Delaware, in a home owned by Hockessin Friends Meeting. In return for free rent, they took care of the graveyard, mostly a matter of mowing the grass. There they raised five children —Richard, Deborah, David, Nancy and Betsy—all of whom, except Deborah, now live on the West Coast. Ken and Carol were kind enough to put me up for several months in 1966, when I was putting my new life in order. Ken and I were both self-taught golfers; we played together a number of times on DuPont's excellent golf course.

In the summer of 1967 the family vacationed in Colorado, with the intention of doing some serious mountain-climbing. My father had died earlier that year, and my mother, who had suffered a serious heart attack several years earlier, went to live in a nursing home near Kenneth. Deborah had remained at home, for reasons now forgotten. I was at Lehigh when I got word from Carol of Ken's shocking death while mountain climbing. I undertook the task of going to Hockessin to break the sad news to Debbie and her grandmother. I recall receiving warm thanks from Carol for my having made the trip.

JOHN BLANCHE

I was born August 22, 1926 in Trenton, New Jersey. I attended Catholic schools until I graduated from Trenton Catholic in 1944. In August of that year I enlisted in the US Navy. My boot camp training was in Sampson, New York. Immediately following boot camp, in December of 1944, I was assigned to the crew of the battleship, *USS Missouri*, in Bayonne, New Jersey. I served on the *Missouri* for 20 months. Though I did not witness the actual signing of the peace treaty, I was one of a crew of 2500 shipmates on board during the formal surrender of Japan to the allied nations. It was, without a doubt, a momentous occasion, bringing to an end the hostilities of World War II.

John Blanche

I was a seaman on a deck force, Division 4, to be exact, that also manned a 5-inch gun mount. I was in the 5-inch gun mount handling-room during all engagements, sending the projectiles up to the gun mount to be loaded into the breach for firing.

We were at sea, off the coast of Japan, when the Japanese surrendered. We then received orders to go into Tokyo Bay for the actual signing of the peace treaty. All the dignitaries were brought aboard by launches for the signing:

John Blanche

General MacArthur, supreme commander for the Allied Powers.

For the United States – Fleet Admiral Chester W. Nimitz.

For the Republic of China – General Hsu Yung Chang.

For the United Kingdom – Admiral Sir Bruce Fraser, GCB, KBE.

For the Union of Soviet Republics – Lieutenant General Kuzma Derevyanko Nikolaevish.

For the Commonwealth of Australia- General Sir Thomas Blamey.

For the Dominion of Canada – Colonel Lawrence Moore-Cosgrave.

For the Provincial Government of the French Republic – Major General Jacques LeClerc (Count Philippe de Hauteclocque).

For the United Kingdom of the Netherlands - Admiral C.E.L. Helfrich.
For the Dominion of New Zealand – Air Marshall, L.M. Isitt, RNZAF.

I didn't see any of the formal ceremonies because the peace treaty was signed on the starboard side, and I was on the port side, manning the rail.

The *USS Missouri*, the last battleship of the Iowa class to be built during World War II, was built by the New York shipyard, and commissioned on June 11, 1944. She arrived in the Pacific in January 1945, and the Ryukyus (Okinawa) a month later. She was instrumental in raids on Japan's homeland, just prior to the end of World War II. In May of 1945 she became the flagship of the Third Fleet and on September 2, 1945 was the site of the Japanese surrender ceremony, which ended World War II. It was a glorious moment.

On one occasion during a kamikaze attack off Okinawa, a suicide plane crashed into the starboard quarter on the main deck, and burst into flames. Fortunately, there was very little damage to the ship, and no one was killed.

Following the end of hostilities, she returned to the United States, for a great naval review in New York in October 1945. In March 1946, she went to the Mediterranean on a diplomatic mission. In the 1940s and the early 1950s she operated in the Atlantic.

The signing of the Peace Treaty, Sept. 2, 1945. General MacArthur on the left.

By June 1950, she was the only US battleship on active duty. She was involved in the Korean War, and several training cruises to Europe. She was decommissioned in 1955, and for three decades was in reserve in Bremerton, Washington. In 1980 she was reactivated along with the Iowa, Wisconsin, and the New Jersey. In May 1986, she was recommissioned for the next six years. During that time she participated in a round-the-world cruise and other activities, including a combat role in the Persian Gulf War in 1991.

Signing: General Yoshijiro Umezu, Chief of the Army General Staff. Watching: Lieutenant General Richard K. Sunderland and General MacArthur.

The "Mighty Mo," as she was sometimes called, was decommissioned for the last time, after almost 50 years, in March of 1992, and in 1995 she was officially stricken from the Naval Vessel Register. Today, one can board the *Missouri* in Hawaii and visit another memorial, dedicated in remembrance of World War II, and the attack on Pearl Harbor.

Frank Blanche, left, with his parents Kathryn and Adam Blanche

Today I live and work for my son-in-law who owns and operates Rice's Market in Lahaska, Pennsylvania. There I work two days a week, and enjoy getting out with people. I enjoy fishing whenever I can, along the New Jersey Coast.

Compiler's Note:

John came from a family of four other brothers, all of whom served in WW II. They are the sons of Adam and Kathryn Blanche, originally from Trenton, New Jersey. Adam, the father, served as a captain in the Trenton Police Department.

Jake served in the U S Coast guard, Pacific
John served in the US Navy, Pacific
Louis served in the US Army, Europe
Pete served in the US Army Air Force,
    Europe
Frank served in the US Navy, Pacific

Jake Blanche

Lou Blanche

Pete Blanche

APPENDIX

The following is adapted from the program for the Dedication of the World War II War Memorial that took place in Washington, D.C. on May 29, 2004:

World War II War Memorial
Democracy over Tyranny
Washington, District of Columbia
United States of America

The Purpose of the Memorial
The Memorial was built to honor the 16 million men and women who served in World War II, including the more than 400,000 who died, and the millions who supported the war effort on the home front.

Introduction
After more than 60 years, a National World War II War Memorial has really been created for those who served in that war. About 60 million people perished in the 2,193 days from the time of the German invasion of Poland in 1939 to the Japanese surrender in Tokyo Bay, September 2, 1945.

Dedication
Beginning at 2:00 P.M. on May 29, 2004, the memorial was dedicated in the presence of 150,000 people, climaxing a campaign that began in 1987. Principal speakers were Tom Brokaw, news commentator and author of the book, "The Greatest Generation Speaks", and Tom Hanks, actor in the movie, "Saving Private Ryan." Each gave a brief presentation, and President George W. Bush was invited to receive the memorial on behalf of the Nation.

Official Ceremony
Presentation of State Flags
U.S. Naval Band

Invocation
Archbishop Philip M. Hannan
World War II Chaplain

General P.X. Kelley, U.S. Marine Corps (ret)
Chairman, American Battle Monument Commission
Presentation of the WW II War Memorial to the Nation

Senator Robert Dole was appointed on March 19, 1997,
National Campaign Chairman
and Frederich W. Smith, National Co-Chairman

Others in Attendance:
Former President William Clinton
Former President George H. W. Bush

Establishing the Construction of the WW II War Memorial

On May 25, 1993 the American Battle Monument Commission was authorized by congress and President Clinton to establish the WW II War Memorial in our Nation's Capital. The Memorial is located on the National Mall in Washington, D.C. between the Lincoln Memorial and the Washington Monument.

Casualties during World War II, 1941 to 1945

Today fewer than 5 million veterans remain alive. A little more than 400,000 veterans lost their lives during the war. More than 16.4 million Americans, both men and women, served in World War II. Those alive today are in their late 70's or older and passing at the rate of 1100 per day.

World-Wide Casualties from WW II related activities, 1939 to 1945

During the period from the German invasion of Poland in 1939 to the surrender of the Japanese aboard the Battleship *USS Missouri* in Tokyo Bay in September1945, an estimated 60 million people perished from war-related activities.

Architect

The architect and designer was Frederich St. Florna, a native of Austria where in the Spring of 1945 he experienced as a boy of 12 what would be his most vivid memory of WW II - the triumphant arrival of American soldiers in his Austrian village.

Sculptor

The sculptor of the granite and bronze memorial was Ray Koskey.

What the Design Stands For

The most distinct symbolisms are the words: "Victory on Land," "Victory at Sea," and "Victory in the Air," on the floor of the arches to celebrate victories in the Atlantic and Pacific theaters.

Ground Breaking

Ground breaking began on November 11, 2000.

Construction

Construction began in August, 2001. It was completed in May of 2004.

Funding and Cost

The funding of the WW II War Memorial was paid for almost entirely by private contributions. A total of $193 million in cash and pledges was raised by individual American corporations, and foundations, veterans' groups, civic groups, professional and fraternal organizations, states and one territory, students, and some 1200 schools. The cost of the Project is currently at $172 million. After these costs are paid, any remaining funds left from the $193 million will be held in a World War II War Memorial trust fund to be used by the American Battle Monument Commission exclusively for the Memorial.

National Park Service

On November 1, 2004, the Memorial was transferred from the American Battle Monument Commission to the National Park Service. The Park service will have the responsibility of its operation and maintenance.

World War II Registry of Remembrances

The World War II Registry of Remembrances will list the names of individual Americans who participated in the war effort, to be recorded for all time in the annals of history. The Registry will be kept in Washington, D.C., so future generations will always remember the sacrifices of America's World War II generation.

The Internet

Almost unlimited information on the WW II War Memorial is available on the internet at www.wwiimemorial.com

A hundred times every day I remind myself that my inner and outer life depends on the labors of other men [and women], living and dead, and that I must exert myself in order to give in the measure as I have received and am still receiving.—Albert Einstein

This photos was taken on 8 June 2005 during a visit by over 350 veterans from Bucks County, Pennsylvania to the World War II Memorial in Washington, D.C. and is presented by Congressman Michael G. Fitzpatrick (PA-08) with his unending thanks and gratitude for their service.

A view of part of Memorial Plaza.

The Atlantic Pavilion with Pillars

The Pacific Pavilion with Pillars.

197

A view of part of Memorial Plaza.

Part of the Memorial Plaza showing the Eisenhower Statement.

INDEX